Healthy Mother, Healthy Child

Creating Whole Families from the Inside Out

ELIZABETH IRVINE

bright sky press
HOUSTON, TEXAS

2365 Rice Boulevard, Suite 202,
Houston, Texas 77005

10   9   8   7   6   5   4   3   2   1

Library of Congress Cataloging-in-Publication Data

Irvine, Elizabeth.
Healthy mother, healthy child : creating whole families from the inside out / Elizabeth Irvine.
p. cm.
ISBN 978-1-933979-82-3 (softcover)
1. Hatha yoga for children. 2. Mother and child. 3. Nutrition. 4. Holistic medicine. I. Title.

RJ133.7I78 2010
613.7'046083—dc22   2009053988

Photos appearing on pages 10, 20, 80, 82, 98, 114, 121, 128, 134, 136, 144 © Karen Walrond
Photos appearing on pages 24, 36, 63, 84, 154, 158, 163 © Karen Sachar
Cover illustration by Mike Guillory
Printed in China through Asia Pacific Offset

Healthy Mother, Healthy Child

Creating Whole Families from the Inside Out

ELIZABETH IRVINE

bright sky press
HOUSTON, TEXAS

Sarah, Allie, and Sam. I love you.

Sarah, Allie, and Sam. I love you.

The Story of the Butterfly

What happens to you when you see a butterfly? For me, a wandering butterfly crossing my path makes me stop in my tracks. Appreciating its beauty, I somehow shift, right then, to a softer focus. Just like that, seeing a butterfly allows me a moment of grace. Use the butterfly that glides through the pages of this book as your touchstone, capturing your attention and reminding you every moment is a chance to create health and happiness on your motherhood journey.

TABLE OF CONTENTS

1

A Balanced Life

It's another routine weekday. Everyone up early, scrambling with the morning ritual of getting children to school and adults to work, all on time. Shoulders are heavy with stress from job deadlines, homework, chaotic after-school activities, and the spin cycle of getting up and doing it all again tomorrow. Simultaneously attempting to plan a quick dinner menu and pack healthy lunches it seems everybody has some kind of complaint: a runny nose, a dull headache, "I can't focus at school," or didn't sleep well. As a mother, it can seem nearly impossible to create health and happiness, not only for yourself but for your whole family. But even though I still have mornings like the one above, I am here to tell you that once you discover health and happiness begins from the inside out, it really is possible to feel good for no reason, everyday. And, it begins through creating a place of capacity, emotional and physical "shock absorbers" to help you and your children withstand everyday challenges through a routine of preventive care. In the end Benjamin Franklin got it right: *"An ounce of prevention is worth a pound of cure."*

For the last fifteen years, the focus of my work has been helping others create a healthy balance in their day-to-day life. And yes, I personally struggle with the same stress, pressure, and not having enough time in the day to squeeze it all in as you do. But I know all too well that the wear and tear of our demanding lifestyles takes its toll on all of us, parents and kids. Our bodies can put up with it only for so long until our stress manifests as a physical or emotional problem, be it the common cold, a headache, insomnia, or a bad mood. Lucky for us, by focusing on prevention—building up our emotional and physical reserves—we can avoid many of those problems entirely, creating families that are wholly happy and healthy in the process.

The body can heal itself

For years, my children and I have played a game whenever we see a FedEx delivery truck. On the side of the truck, imbedded in the letters "FedEx," there is an arrow incorporated into the logo. You have to look at the words in a different way—soften your gaze and see past the letters to find the arrow resting inside. My kids could always spot it right away, laughing their heads off, "Aw come on, Mom—you can't see it?!" as the truck sped away before I could find it. And then one day, sitting in a long line of going-nowhere traffic, a FedEx truck pulled up next to me. Having nothing else to claim my attention, I relaxed, looking into those letters, and the arrow somehow emerged clear as day. Now

that I know how to look at those letters, I see the arrow right away; it just took that first time to "get it." Our health and happiness are the very same, with children probably more aware of their innate healing ability than we are. It's just like stepping back and seeing our body and its relationship to ourselves, to others, and our world with gentle eyes—allowing our true self, our true wellbeing—to come forward more energy, clarity, strength, and joy. It is always there, just not always seen: our body's own ability to self-heal, to stay in balance and create health and happiness from the inside out.

Dr. Andrew Weil, MD, graduate of Harvard Medical School, director of integrative medicine at the University of Arizona, and probably one of America's best-known doctors, says so accurately in his book *Spontaneous Healing,* "I have titled my book *Spontaneous Healing* because I want to call attention to the innate, intrinsic nature of the healing process. The body can heal itself. It can do so because it has a healing system. At every level of biological organization, from DNA up, self-repair and regeneration exist in us."

My initial journey in discovering the body's ability to self-heal began in London with a sick baby. While my family was living in England, my son Sam developed severe allergies that led me to search for a wider knowledge, a deeper understanding of the roots of disease. The top medical experts had told me that Sam's condition was unfixable, and that the only treatment was to try and ease the symptoms and keep him comfortable. As a nurse, I understood the language of conventional medicine; as a mother, I knew this answer was unacceptable. Over the years, Sam and I learned about a more natural way of living—simple but powerful tools of food, yoga, relaxation, and myriad other ways of allowing the body to self-heal. Through Sam's recovery, I learned to walk a new, gray line that accepts both conventional medicine and complementary medicine as helpful and necessary. My son's challenge became my portal that led me to a place of new possibilities and the discovery of a new way of caring for his little body, and my own.

In 2003, my family returned to the United States after living abroad for fifteen years. After only a few days in the humid, allergen-laden Houston air, Sam had an asthma attack. Luckily, a precautionary "emergency" inhaler quickly dilated the bronchi in his lungs, and he recovered. Based on my experience when he was a baby, I also realized that in this city, our new home, we were going to need some help to keep Sam's body in balance. My first stop was locating a couple of good complementary practitioners who practiced natural medicine—an acupuncturist and a homeopath. This was followed by a trip to the grocery store to stock up on fresh food and naturally "allergy-proofing" his bedroom. Within less than a week, Sam was back to normal and breathing easy.

> Through Sam's recovery, I learned to walk a new, gray line that accepts both conventional medicine and complementary medicine.

When I reach past my reflection in the mirror of my medicine cabinet to what lies behind the door, on those glass shelves I find an array of herbs, medicinal products, and conventional medications. The combination allows me to care for my body, all the while remaining true to the most basic doctrine of medical law: "First, do no harm."

With twenty-five years' experience as a health care professional, as a mother, and as a teacher of healthy living, I feel that I now serve as a translator, interpreting from one language, one health system to another. I speak and respect both the language of complementary medicine—such as Ayurveda, acupuncture, homeopathy—and conventional medicine. Returning to the U.S. and seeing how we Americans use conventional medicine—as a magic bullet enabling us to keep up with the pace of society—was a culture shock. Initially, I felt alone in a place that was supposed to feel familiar. However, what ultimately felt right was a "knowingness" allowing me to stand firmly in my belief of holistic health and happiness. Today in the dawn of America's new healthcare overhaul— our crippling problems with costs, childhood obesity, and the fear of interdependence on a fragile system—I am reminded of those first few weeks after returning back home, returning to a place that felt uncomfortably foreign for me.

There are many ways to create a disease-free, healthy life. As a mother, dealing with the illness of my own baby, I had to leave no stone unturned. Conventional medicine saves lives every day. If one of my children breaks an arm, we go straight to the emergency room, or if one has an ear infection, I will use antibiotics. However, both of these examples involve fixing the body in crisis; I encourage you to create wellness—to prevent illness before it occurs. In ancient Asia, people paid a doctor for a healthy checkup and went for free if they became sick. Imagine if we could switch our emphasis to prevention! How many health care providers would jump on the bandwagon and turn their practices into well-being centers—not a bad idea.

I feel my unique professional and personal experience in fusing modern technology with thousands of years of natural wisdom—simple yet powerful remedies of food, increased self-awareness, and a sundry of options—which allow me to build a bridge for you, to connect and introduce you to concepts other than the magic bullet. I want them to become familiar instead of strange, bringing you confidence to try them and incorporate some of them into your life on a regular basis, building your family's emotional and physical capacity.

By maintaining a higher standard of health and wellness, we not only raise the quality of our day-to-day lives, we also take the pressure off our current health care system. When you are empowered to reach beyond the boundaries of conventional medicine as a quick fix and reclaim the wisdom lying dormant in your own body, you will find yourself both healthier and happier, and feel your interconnectedness to our world. The water I drink, the air I breathe, the food I eat, and the sun that shines on my face are part of me and I am part of them. And, as a mother leading my family in living a greener life, I teach them this sacred connection and the responsibility of caring for our ecosystem. For me, the wisdom I have gained about the true nature of wellness is reflected both in the objects on the glass shelves of my medicine cabinet and in the face I see in the mirror.

Ok, you say, I'm ready. So where do I begin? To begin focusing on prevention, you must first recognize the link between stress and physical health, and one of the first steps in managing stress is to become aware of it. How many times at the end of the day do you sit back and think about how you felt during the day? Did you feel rushed? Tired? Angry? Overwhelmed? Frustrated? Just plain cranky? Recognizing your feelings is a huge step on the path to controlling them.

Learning to use yoga, breathing, and relaxation as "remedies" can help you combat the battle of stress and all its negative side effects. If you learn how to incorporate some sort of relaxation practice into your life, it can give your body the opportunity to perform as the amazing machine that it is. Why do I say it starts with you, and not with your kids? Because as women, we set the tone. Women are often compared to Mother Earth; we ground and center the home, nurturing each family member's body and soul.

According to Dr. Christine Northrup, noted author of *Women's Bodies Women's Wisdom,* "The female energy system—centripetal energy—is the grounding force that affects everyone around us … when a woman changes her life for the better, her entire family benefits. The wellbeing of the family and of society itself depends upon women becoming and remaining healthy. Part of creating health is understanding the power of female energy and its implications. The health of a woman's loved ones is directly linked to her own personal health. So we owe it to ourselves first to take the time we need to heal." The first step is helping yourself; the next step is passing on the benefit to your children.

> The first step is helping yourself; the next step is passing the benefit on to your children.

Stress buster

Let's get started with an easy technique to reduce some physical stress and bring balance and wellbeing into your every day. Once you practice the following "stress buster" for your spine a few times, you can put this concept in your back pocket and pull it out anytime you need a break in your day. Forget about fitness fads, and let's get back to basics. I like to start with something simple and effortless to incorporate into your every day.

I bring my awareness to my breath

and notice my inhalation and my

exhalation—and taking in a few slow

deep breaths and releasing them back

out as I allow my rib cage to expand, my

breath gently soothes and nurtures

my body's posture. Try it now.

How does it make you feel?

Powerhouse connection

I am always talking about my spine, my master connector. It works hard carrying my arms and legs around, holding my head in place—it allows me to sit, stand, and bend. It connects all my nerves and pathways to my body's organs. It's the power strip of my body. Can you imagine yourself without a healthy backbone? One important tool in keeping your body healthy is to treat the core of your body with respect.

Practice this anytime, anywhere

Here is a simple, tried-and-true technique that I have taught to thousands of people who want to begin to take good care of their bodies. The beauty of this practice is it can be done anytime, anywhere—and no one else even needs to know what you are doing. This is how I do it. Standing or sitting—I think about my feet, and place them hip-width apart feeling equally balanced weight on both of my feet—heavy and grounded in my feet. Now I allow my attention to travel up to my pelvis and feel the spreading and widening of my pelvis as my body begins to respond by lining up with my feet and correcting my posture. The ripple continues up to my shoulders, as if they automatically draw back and down and away from my ears, rolling back, allowing more space for my chest to be open and free. I keep my head and neck in line with my spine, and imagine a jewel resting upon the crown of my head, allowing me to hold my head with dignity and poise. I bring my awareness to my breath and notice my inhalation and my exhalation—and taking a few slow deep breaths in and releasing them back out as I allow my rib cage to expand, my breath gently soothes and nurtures my body's posture. Try it now. How does it make you feel?

This beautiful and natural position for my body allows my spine to be relaxed, and it takes out the kinks and ensures a better interconnection with my body. A great first step toward wellness is to do this systematic approach with your body regularly throughout the day. When your spine is held with a relaxed grace it not only creates a feeling of beauty, dignity, and confidence, it allows a powerful response in connecting you to your natural ability to be healthy.

Chapter 1: A Balanced Life

LET'S TALK

Typically, after I finish a lecture, I allow time for Q&A. I'm a straight talker, and during this time I've found some of the best information seems to come forth, organically. Even though we aren't physically in the same room together, let's pretend we are. I've dedicated the "Let's Talk" section in each chapter to questions that may be percolating in the back of your mind after reading the material. Following are a few questions that may resonate with you, and help you apply the previous chapter's ideas into your everyday.

Q: *What's one thing I can do tomorrow to begin to create a healthy balanced life?*

A: Specifically, look at your day-to-day life and start small. By focusing on prevention and building on these changes slowly and gradually, you'll have lasting effects. Whether that means dedicating five minutes a day to relaxing, dropping off the recycling once a week, or eating a piece of fruit instead of a candy bar, making one change toward preventive health and wellbeing makes a difference. Remember, too, that your children will follow in your positive example.

Q: *What's the difference between conventional medicine and alternative medicine, and why do I care?*

A: To create a healthy lifestyle with lasting effects, "working from the inside out" is the concept to remember. Alternative therapies often look to the root of the problem, while conventional medicine treats the symptoms of disease. I encourage you to use a combination of both of these modalities. Use alternative therapies to prevent these issues from developing and conventional methods to treat an acute problem if your body gets into a crisis. **Accept both modalities** and let them complement each other, fusing modern technology with thousands of years of natural wisdom. Use your food, increased self awareness, a sundry of options—and build a bridge for you to connect and introduce you to concepts other than the "magic bullet". In doing so you'll keep yourself well with the bonus of taking the pressure off our current health care system.

Q: *Sometimes I feel just plain cranky, tired, overwhelmed, or frustrated. What am I supposed to do?*

A: The single most important thing you can do to deal with any of these emotions, is to RECOGNIZE what you are feeling. If you don't recognize the problem, how can you possibly fix it? Once you acknowledge this sensation you are already on your way to positive change.

Q: *I know relaxation is a huge part of letting my body heal, but I just don't know how.*

A: Start with the simple body and breathing awareness technique described in this chapter. You can practice this anytime, anywhere, and it only takes a few minutes. Remember to think like a princess: hold your spine with dignity and confidence, bring your awareness to your body, take a relaxing deep breath in and out. Connect to your natural ability to be healthy and your body will respond. And, remember, as mothers, we set the tone. Your good habits send beautiful ripples to everyone you are near.

2

Nourishing Body and Soul

The other day I took the time to take my car in for service and an oil change. What a pain, I thought, as I drove to our local garage. It was a busy morning and I nearly decided to put it off to another day, but ultimately stuck to my plan. While sitting an hour in a mechanic's greasy waiting area is not my idea of fun, I regularly take the time to service my car, fuel it up, keep it clean, and ensure it's safe to drive. I know that if I make the effort I will be rewarded with a dependable car that takes me where I need to go. Honestly, my body is the very same. If I do the regular maintenance I stay physically and mentally healthy—and I'm then able to use my body to the best of its ability. So many of us don't think twice about getting our cars' regular oil changes, but won't take any time out to contribute to our own body's routine maintenance.

High maintenance

The creation of a healthy lifestyle requires a multi-faceted approach that includes many ideas in this book: caring for your whole body, physically, emotionally, and spiritually. Included in this overall plan is the regular maintenance a healthy body needs. Breathing and body awareness, relaxation, adequate sleep, as well as developing sound nutritional habits all fit together to prevent stress. In this chapter, I want to focus on that last one. Let's face it, the food we eat affects us enormously emotionally and physically, and forms an intricate link in our overall health. Socrates puts it simply, "Let your food be your medicine, and medicine be your food." The good news is that the food we eat is within our control and nutrition is an area where small, gradual changes tangibly improve how we look and feel everyday. Equating our bodies with our cars, in properly managing our bodies' fuel we need to focus on premium quality, listen and notice how our machine is humming along, as well as being mindful of when our tanks are running on empty. The bottom line: You require regular maintenance, and carving out the time isn't always easy, but you are worth the effort.

TWO KEY POINTS: WHAT AND HOW

Forming good nutritional habits doesn't happen overnight. Following are two key points that can turn your new healthy lifestyle into reality. Start slow and gradually build on these critical foundations: WHAT do I feed my body, and HOW do I take in my nourishment?

WHAT YOU EAT

What do I feed my body, and how do I take in my nourishment?

Back in my nursing days, I loved nothing more than to grab a glazed donut and a cup of coffee to keep me going. It was a quick fix that I thought would take me through the endless tasks ahead of me. I now realize that the sugar-and-caffeine high felt fantastic for a short while, but later left me nowhere to go but down as the effects wore off and I became irritable and hungry. Food culprits leading to low blood sugar include items like my donuts and coffee; the snack was high in sugar, refined white flour, and hydrogenated fat, combined with an overdose of caffeine. Alternatively, eating foods high in protein and complex carbohydrates—easy to do if you eat food in its most natural state—gives you stamina and keeps you on an even keel. How much better I would have felt if I had substituted a piece of cheese and whole-meal crackers, or fruit and nuts eaten at regular intervals during my day. Based on my experience and gained knowledge, nowadays I am able to make good, healthy choices that give me increased energy, an even temperament, and contribute to an overall healthy diet.

Plain and simple, good food makes you feel great

Through years of watching my healthy eating and developing their own habits, my kids have come to understand how much better healthy food makes them feel. It is something that has evolved since they were quite young. When they were little, we lived in the countryside on the outskirts of London; consequently, they weren't exposed to fast food. When we arrived back in the U.S. the girls were young teens. Inevitably, perhaps, the girls started to slip into the habit of going with friends to get fast food. The good news is they came to understand on their own that even though this food tasted good while they were eating it, a few hours later they didn't feel so good, just as I felt after eating those glazed donuts. The foundation of good nutrition is becoming attentive to the choices we make about our food and how that food makes us feel. In regard to our children, our own healthy example leads them more clearly and effortlessly than any words you can say.

The first step in making changes is to notice. Can you recognize how you feel a couple of hours after you eat? What does eating a candy bar do for you, or drinking a soda? What effect does a yogurt parfait with granola and fruit have? How is your mood, your appetite throughout your day? You may want to keep a food journal for a week or so to notice your moods and the physical effects of your diet. The first step in changing nutritional habits is recognizing what is wrong; the next is putting one foot forward toward change.

3 FOODS TO AVOID AND 3 FOODS TO INCLUDE IN YOUR SHOPPING BASKET

Put it in:

- **Buy fresh:** Fresh foods are located along the outer edges of the grocery store. Stay on the periphery of the store when you shop. Only occasionally enter into the inner aisles where the more processed food is located.
- **Buy seasonal:** Stock up on seasonal fruit and veggies.
- **Buy whole foods:** Avoid processed or artificial ingredients—buy foods in their most natural form.

Put it back:

- **Processed foods** contain these ingredients:
  - Hydrogenated oils
  - Sugar and high fructose corn syrup
  - Enriched or bleached flour

HOW YOU EAT

Why bother?

A deep swallow and I realize the last bite of my oatmeal is gone. Unfortunately, my first clue is hearing the spoon scraping the bottom of the bowl and not the satisfying feeling from what I ate. How often do you eat a meal without noticing what you just ate? How many times have you eaten on the run as you chase a toddler, or put food in your mouth staring at your computer screen at your desk?

It seems too simple. Slow down and notice the taste; chew until your mouth is empty, then wait for your stomach to send a message back to your brain saying that it's full. Even if your food choice is healthy, eating without attention deprives your body of the proper signals it needs to help you process your food—such as the creation of saliva-producing digestive enzymes. In the end, you can end up with indigestion as well as no memory of your meal. The food we eat is important, but how we eat our food holds a lot of "weight" in our plan.

NOURISHING BODY AND SOUL

A clog in the works

According to Dr. Anthony Cichoke, author of the *Complete Book of Enzyme Therapy*, the effects of poor digestion go beyond a little tummy ache. In fact, "digestion is the mechanism that makes your body work . . . a clog in the works may be only the tip of the iceberg, because poor digestion interferes with nutrient breakdown, absorption and metabolism; allows toxins to remain in the body and accumulate; and over-stresses the body." To sum it up, poor digestion is a synonym for poor nutrition. Even if you are eating fresh, seasonal, whole foods and avoiding processed foods, when your digestive system isn't working properly, your body isn't able to absorb what it needs. Additionally, it is difficult to lose weight or feel your best if you have poor digestion. According to Dr. Cichoke, "Improper digestion is usually the cause of most weight problems. Poor digestion takes a lot out of your body, and makes it weak, leaving it more vulnerable to attacks from other sources."

RAW FOODS TO HELP WITH DIGESTION

Ultimately, slowing down and being mindful of your food is a huge step in allowing your food to digest properly and to aid you in eating appropriate amounts of food. Including some raw fruits or veggies at every meal can also help with improving your digestion.

Try out some of these naturally enzyme-rich foods:

- Fermented foods, such as yogurt or kefir
- Fruit juice
- Soy sauce
- Pineapple
- Avocado
- Artichoke

I have very clear childhood memories of sitting around the dinner table with my family of seven. My dad would turn on the chandelier over the table to set the mood; when the "tranquility light" was on, all five of us kids understood this meant the room was to be peaceful. A thankful prayer for food and family was followed by a general chat about our day. No one asked to be excused until the meal was finished and the conversation naturally came to an end.

Make it a priority

Does that dinner scenario sound difficult to do in this day and age? Though times are different, now that I am the parent, I make a clear effort for that type of family meal to be a priority. Families who eat together nourish body and soul. Food is meant to bring our bodies the energy they need, but equally important is our need to nourish our emotional wellbeing. What better combination than good, comforting food and being with the people who care so much for you?

The demands of work schedules, children's extra activities, and just being too tired to deal with preparing dinner may be some reasons regular family dinners may not be happening right now in your house. Those demands aside, when as parents we prioritize where it is we really want to spend our time, we might find the energy to organize a regular family meal.

Family night

On a busy day—most days, I would guess—mealtime can be the only time a family gets to spend together, and this connection is vital. If you are not already eating together every night, take a weekend night and make it "family night," reserved for dinner with the family. Plan a menu that appeals to everyone. Set the table in the dining room or put a cloth on the kitchen table. Use candles, flowers, anything to make it special. Create a mood for dinner that is something out of the ordinary and make your family the guests. You might begin with a drink before dinner—my children loved having juice or ginger ale in a special glass when they were little—and take a few minutes to relax together. Relaxing into your meal sets the tone for your evening and for good digestion. Start off the meal with an expression of thanks and gratitude for the food and each other. Promote good manners. Children learn what they observe, so lead the way using good etiquette and your children will never have to worry about proper table manners when they begin to eat outside the home.

Another important aspect of the family meal, other than connection, is how much your children actually absorb—intellectually—around the table. Try to keep the conversation at dinner engaging. Conversation doesn't have to be about or directed to the children, but the more they can join in, the better. Harvard University studies link children's literacy and school success to explanatory talk at the dinner table. Topics like politics or stories from the daily news can expand a child's world. It can also help them handle differences of opinion, negotiate ways to get into the conversation, and hear new vocabulary.

Assuming parents are not going to argue or bring up a topic that should be discussed privately, a routine family meal provides a life skill and a wonderful sense of security for children. For our family, sharing a meal puts us all in a better mood. Sometimes you can almost see the tension rising as we orchestrate the food, drink, and everyone sitting down together. However, what an amazing oasis of calm rolls in after everyone has some food in their tummy and a little conversation.

TIPS TO MAKE THIS A REALITY

- **Start small.** Aim for one family meal a week and then build. Set a goal of how many nights a week you would like to eat as a family; you'll be amazed at how often you get there.

- **Make one meal.** Perhaps children can add or take away an ingredient such as different toppings for pasta or pizza, yet everyone eats the same. No special orders keeps it simple, and most kids actually prefer to eat like everyone else.

- **Every meal doesn't have to be a banquet.** Fresh take-out food or a quick bag of pasta and a jar of sauce go a long way toward pulling dinner together and ensuring you are all eating it together.

- **Make meals a joint effort.** Find a job for everyone. Even small children can contribute to a meal. Simple tasks such as laying napkins or cutlery, or carrying the salt and pepper to the table all help and give the feeling of working together. Ditto for cleaning up. The famous expression "many hands make light work" is a mantra in our house.

- **Maybe a family dinner is out of the question.** Why not try another meal? Breakfast can work if you get up a little earlier. Experiment with some options.
- **If it's too late for little ones** to wait for a working parent to get home in the evening, save a course (such as dessert) and they can eat it along with you.

The rituals we make for our families can make lasting impressions for our children. Look what happened to me!

Reading between the lines

It all started at the grocery store with a package of corn chips. My daughter Allie was just learning to read and, as a young budding reader, was fascinated by all the strange words on the back of the bag. She tried reading the ingredients then looked up at me and asked, "Mommy, what's 'red 40' and 'yellow 6?'" I told her those were colorings that the manufacturer puts into the chips. Her precious young face looked stricken. "What are colors doing in this package of chips?" she asked. I replied by telling her the truth: These artificial colors are made from chemicals and these dyes are used to make the food look more attractive, but have nothing to do with making the chips more healthy. In fact, just the opposite was true. I told her there is lots of research to prove that these unnatural things are not very good for us. With a look of disgust, she walked back and placed the chips on the shelf. She picked up another bag, studied the label for a while, and without saying a word placed it back on the rack. Then she continued on down the aisle and walked straight over to a display of fruit, picked up an orange, and placed it in the basket.

Never again did she ask for those chips. She figured it out on her own, with a little guidance, and it took the pressure off me. Educating and guiding your children to take ownership empowers them to make their own healthy choices. Teach your kids to notice how good food makes them feel so, in time, the right choice will come from within. Parents are the most important influence when it comes to a child's nutrition. Honestly, as I mentioned earlier, nothing is better than leading through example.

Eat the food before you need it.

Try this healthy breakfast experiment:

Serve protein and whole grain for

breakfast. Take one morning and serve

two of these choices: eggs, nut butter,

whole-grain toast, whole-grain cereals

with no added sugar, soy milk, yogurt, or

fresh fruit. See for yourself. Notice how you

feel later in the day, watch how your kids

respond with better mood and attention.

Commonsense approach

In a study on nutrition and human behavior conducted by Dr. Neil Ward at the University of Surrey in England—problems such as hyperactivity, excessive allergy, and dyslexia were markedly improved by modifying a child's diet and supplementing with vitamins and minerals. Nutrition and vitamins, used as the only intervention, got better results than similar studies that used pharmaceuticals.

Another convincing study supports a commonsense approach to nutrition. This study involved 3,000 young offenders who experienced a 70 to 80 percent reduction in criminal behavior over twelve months while on a high-nutrition diet.

STICK TO THE BASICS

We take care of the things we love, and our body is no exception. Speaking nutritionally, sticking to basics keeps it plain and simple.

- **Natural, seasonal, wholesome foods taste good**—once your body gets accustomed to them. And, eventually your body actually adjusts to craving healthy foods.

- **Learn to read a label.** Teach your child to read labels—if they can't pronounce an ingredient, it probably isn't natural or the best choice.

- **Eat more foods without a label!** Make fresh whole foods the biggest part of what you eat.

- **Eat foods that give a steady, even flow of energy.** Complex carbohydrates (such as whole grains) and protein (cheese, meat, eggs) provide a daylong release of energy.

- **Avoid sugar and highly processed foods.**

- **Avoid chemicals, dyes, and preservatives.** Numerous studies prove additives can cause violent bouts of hyperactivity in children. Phosphates (found in processed foods such as hot dogs, processed cheese) and other preservatives are linked to numerous problems with allergies and behavior.

Rome wasn't built in a day

Before my son's illness sparked change, I was probably the leader in my family when it came to poor eating. That donut-and-coffee habit developed from my many years of staff nursing. Speaking from experience, it is easier to start with small changes and gradually build to a healthier style. It's unrealistic to change your diet or your child's diet drastically and forbid all of those not-so-nutritious foods. In my family, it's a constant work in progress. Rome wasn't built in a day, as they say; however, we now typically eat fresh, seasonal foods in their most natural state and junk food is not the norm.

Yes, some days it is hard to choose healthy food over convenience. There are so many choices when it comes to feeding our bodies; when we are overloaded with choices, it is difficult to make the right one. I feel the key is to keep it simple. Apply the words "fresh, seasonal, whole, natural" to the foods you eat, and be mindful of how and when you eat. If you use these simple guidelines as your touchstones in building healthy eating habits, in return your family's total health will be the reward, for generations to come.

HOW DO YOU FEEL?

After you eat, you should feel better. If instead you feel tired or irritable, depressed, congested, or bloated, you probably didn't eat the right food for you—no matter how fresh. If certain foods seem to cause you real discomfort or symptoms, see the information on allergies in Chapter 5 for more information on the foods that trigger the most allergic responses.

10 TIPS FOR EATING HEALTHY

Keep food simple and natural.

Vary the type of food with respect to the season.

Create a habitual time for eating your meals.

Pay attention to how you eat.

Take a moment of quiet gratitude before you eat.

Look at your food, notice how it tastes, chew, and enjoy!

Avoid fast food restaurants.

Ask yourself, will this food benefit my body?

Lead your children by a healthy example.

Enjoy and have fun with creating and eating meals.

PERSONAL EXAMPLES FROM MY FAMILY'S KITCHEN

Get your kids involved in the kitchen. Even a four-year-old can add ingredients to a pot or bowl. Homemade pizza dough can be tons of fun for kids to make. Older children can help with menu planning. My kids make a list of their favorite meals to incorporate into our weekly menu.

Vary the presentation. Veggies don't have to come with dinner. My kids love raw carrots with lots of "dip" while dinner is being prepared and they're starving. Vegetables sautéed in butter can be more appealing than steamed or boiled.

A multivitamin and mineral supplement made from a food source allows excellent absorption. Choose one that supplies all the RDAs plus zinc and essential fatty acids.

Junk food alternatives:

- Rice crackers, pretzels, or natural chips without any additives replace chips.
- Fresh fruit, dried fruits, and nuts replace candy.
- Homemade cakes, muffins with carrot or apple, or natural cereal bars replace store-bought cakes and cookies.
- Juice without additives, or sugar combined with sparkling water instead of soda.
- Chopped veggies with hummus replace chips and dip.

Chapter 2: Nourishing Body and Soul

Q: *Some days I eat really healthy, and other days I simply fall off the wagon. What can you suggest to help?*

A: It is essential to understand the importance of routine "maintenance" for your body, and food is a big part of that. Socrates puts it simply, "Let food be your medicine and medicine be your food." Once you get into the healthy habit of eating fresh, seasonal, whole foods more often, your body actually begins to crave those foods instead of junk. (Really, it's a process that evolves naturally. And believe me, there was a stage in my life when I loved glazed donuts!)

Q: *What do I look for when I'm shopping to help me get started with a healthy diet?*

A: Here are some of my favorite tips. Think about these ideas next time you make a run to the grocery store.

- **Fresh:** Fresh foods are located along the outer edges of the grocery store.
- **Seasonal:** Stock up on seasonal fruit and veggies.
- **Whole food:** Avoid processed foods or artificial ingredients.
- **Read labels:** Remember, if you can't pronounce a word in the ingredient list, it's probably not the best choice. Eat more foods with less labels!

Q: *I tend to gulp my food down. Why is that bad for me?*

A: Besides the obvious fact that you didn't take any pleasure from your food, your poor digestion goes beyond a little tummy ache. Toxins remain in your body and accumulate, which stresses your body.

Q: *How can I get my children to eat healthy?*

A: It starts with your own decisions around food. As a mother, once you begin to become attentive to the choices you make, your own healthy choices lead your children. Try this healthy breakfast experiment: Serve protein and whole grain: a whole-grain cereal with milk or eggs and whole grain toast. See for yourself. Notice how you feel later in the day, and watch how your kids respond with better mood and attention.

Q: *Having a family meal sounds great, but I don't think it would ever work for my family's busy lifestyle. Does it really make that big a difference anyway? What do you suggest I do to make it happen?*

A: Eating together as a family has positive research to back it up. Harvard University studies link children's literacy and school success to explanatory talk at the dinner table. Family meals also provide a wonderful sense of security for our children, not to mention the health benefits that good digestion and positive feelings that food and good conversation bring. Make it a priority. Set your intention and dedicate your energy to making it happen. Remember, a family meal doesn't have to be dinner. Be creative about when you all can gather. Refer back to this chapter's TIPS TO MAKE THIS A REALITY (page 28) for other hints to get you going.

3

Yoga: Body Awareness, Breathing, and Meditation

I have been teaching different aspects of breathing, body awareness, relaxation, and visualization for nearly twenty years now. It all began when I became involved with teaching childbirth education classes at the hospital. My twin daughters were toddlers and I wanted to be home with them during the day. I decided to become trained in teaching childbirth education classes so that I could teach classes in the evening when my husband was home.

That's when it connected for me: I learned how to use my body awareness and breathing to create a natural ease, a new feeling within me, more relaxed and content. I then understood how to help soon-to-be parents partner together to create a calm environment and how to help the mother use her focused attention, breathing and body awareness in her childbirth experience.

My son Sam's birth was a natural childbirth experience—toward the very end of my labor and his delivery, of course, I changed my mind—but within minutes he was born. The arrival of my son's beautiful body and the amazing response my own body displayed seemed nothing short of a miracle. As I was able to have a natural birth experience, my body created enormous amounts of feel-good chemicals in my very own body's organic pharmacy. Due to his safe arrival and my surplus of endorphins I was on cloud nine. Within thirty minutes after his birth I got up from the delivery table, used the bathroom, washed my face, and asked when I could take him home.

That was the beginning for me of understanding the true nature, the depths of my body's capability to perform when allowed to do what it is capable of. Within the next year I became involved with yoga. Yoga helped me understand in more depth how to use breathing, body awareness, and relaxation to open up to the intrinsic nature of my own body more often.

I tend to help people who need "de-stressing" just naturally. One of my specialties in helping mothers and children create a healthy lifestyle is teaching preventive methods for keeping their body well. Teaching them how to let go of anxiety, stress, and tension shows them how to bring their bodies into a safe, restful cocoon. It also gives their bodies permission to function as they were designed and use their self-healing capability. My role is not that of a nurse in these cases, but that of facilitator; I am the spark to ignite what is already there.

Why yoga?

The practice of yoga is thought to be around 5,000 years old. A yogini—a woman who practices yoga—awakens the union of her body, mind, and spirit, bringing her closer to her true nature and into alignment with her divinity. Yoga is not a religion; you don't have to chant mantras or belong to a certain faith to practice. Instead, yoga is an ancient science that leads to health and wellbeing from the inside out.

The physical practice of yoga is only one part of what are called the eight limbs of yoga. In the Yoga Sutras of Patanjali—the foundation of yoga practice—yoga is described as an eight-limb tree whose branches are moral and ethical codes of conduct. Through restraint, observance, posture, breath control, sense withdrawal, concentration, meditative absorption and *samdhi*—the ultimate purity and joy in being—that eventually help us obtain liberation from life's challenges. Through yoga we can put behind things such as anger and greed or desire and worry, liberating us to ultimate joy and wellbeing. Through my years of continual practice, yoga slowly created subtle changes in me, until eventually it permeated its way through me, bringing balance and harmony to my thoughts, words and actions.

MUCH MORE THAN ON THE MAT

"Hatha" yoga describes any physical practices of yoga, and its **five main principles are proper relaxation, exercise and breathing, diet, positive thinking, and meditation.** In the practice of yoga, I became more aware of my body, more in touch physically and emotionally. It involved simple things, such as noticing how I hold my body's posture or what I ate and how it made me feel. Over time, it became a holistic way of caring for my body that enhances a feeling of well-being and self-esteem. It is a discipline that teaches concentration, encouraging my mind to focus on one thing and bring me a greater sense of clarity. A master of yoga, B.K.S. Iyengar, says that "the light that yoga sheds on life is something special. It is transformative. It does not change the way we see things; it transforms the person who sees. It brings knowledge and elevates it to wisdom."

For me, yoga is much more than the time spent on my mat. **It is about living my yoga, which means incorporating these principles into my everyday life and experiences.** The true essence of this practice—the bringing together of body and mind—connects me to my divine spark and lets me flow in the spirit of God. It is then that I am truly practicing yoga.

Yoga is not about making only our bodies healthy, strong and flexible; it teaches us to make ourselves healthy, strong and flexible.

— Swami Chidanand Saraswatiji

Although there are many different styles of yoga, nearly all styles grow from similar roots grounded in Hatha yoga. In Sanskrit "HA" means sun and "THA" means moon. Hatha is the yoga of balancing these opposing forces. It is the yoga of physical wellbeing. Hatha yoga uses postures, breathing, and meditation to purify the mind, body, and spirit.

Style of yoga

If you have ever looked into a yoga class or yoga practice you may have seen or heard these words: Astanga, Iyengar, or Viniyoga. These are the names of students of Krishnamacharya, known as the father of modern yoga; other classic styles come from the guru Sivananda. If all of these syllables are making your head spin what you need to know is what makes these styles different is emphasis. Some traditions place the emphasis on the strict alignment of the body, while others focus on the coordination of breath and body movement or the flow from one posture to another.

Not all yoga fits into a classic category. Teachers may have trained under more than one tradition and then fused their interpretation into a different "style." A yoga class can vary from a heat-induced strenuous physical workout to a gentle meditative relaxation. No one style is superior to another. Think about what fits you, and you've found the right style. My own practice has evolved into a fusion of my teachers' styles—from my formal yoga education with the Bihar School in India to my practice in the tradition of the late Vanda Scaravelli. Whichever style you choose, take your time and be mindful of your choice, for the rewards can last a lifetime.

MY PRACTICE

Quality of attention

An essential part of my practice is gathering up all my attention and focusing it on the task at hand. I am cultivating a diligent state of mind, beginning with a grounded "coming-home" feeling, back to the gentle primordial rhythm of my breath. I welcome my breath as a gateway to lead me into the movement. It's not about imposing a position upon my body and then breathing—it's the other way around. When I'm completely focused on my breath, my body becomes pliable, just waiting to unfold, it is a true innate response to my "getting out of my own way" and letting my body and breath lead.

The late Vanda Scaravelli, author of *Awakening the Spine,* instructs us not to fight our bodies, but to "drop that heavy load. Do not kill the instinct of the body for the glory of the pose. Listen to your body, watch it, observe its needs, its requests, and even have fun. Play with it as children do. The body has its own intelligence and is willing to cooperate; one only has to have patience and attention. To be sensitive is to be alive."

It's all about attitude

In one word, I feel the biggest message in yoga is "attitude." For me, it's all about being awake and paying attention to my body. When I listen to my body's inner intelligence and let my "inner knowing" take over and guide me, it knows what to do. It's like a spark that ignites, coming into unison with my body, reestablishing contact. Things begin to kick in, and I catch a glimpse of the endless possibilities and knowledge that my body instinctively holds within. Everyone has the capability—it's just about opening up to the opportunity. This ability is innate. I give you the guidelines, but the destination is always found on our own. Through this style of teaching, I realized that the only way to understand was to allow my instincts to take over. My feet or hands become very strong and feel alive, sensing the gravity from the earth. Within my breath I "make space" for my spine to be free, and move in ways I didn't think were possible, similar to how a flower grows up through a crack in the cement. I begin to see myself as a natural growing being that, when given the chance to be free, can respond with amazing clarity.

> Everyone has the capability — it's just about opening up to the opportunity.

Being still and listening

For me, a fundamental approach to yoga is that all poses are ultimately practiced in the same way. It's really a very ingenuous, natural way of working—it doesn't matter if you're in dog pose or headstand, the same principles apply. Another aspect of my practice is to focus on a little part of my body, such as a tiny space in the middle of my shoulder blades. It is an amazing feeling to release tension from subtle and minute places. I don't think I feel anything, but later realize how much tension has eased—working from the inside out. After a pose I rest, staying alert and focused on the positive responses my body instinctively creates. Being still, watching, waiting, and listening are such important parts of my practice.

Communion with spirit

In this quiet, still space, a communion with spirit is easier. This interconnectedness gives my body permission to be in a state of freedom—true wellbeing, a state of healing. Making this connection fills me up. It gives me more than energy; it generates a steadiness for maneuvering my life.

A FEW THINGS TO REMEMBER WHEN PRACTICING YOGA

Physical body: Eating should be light or minimal two hours prior to practicing. Never over-hold a posture, or overstretch, as yoga should never hurt. Bare feet and a non-slip surface are the only equipment you need.

Breathing: Breathe as naturally as possible. Do not force your breath or hold it. Breathe slowly through your nose, with your mouth lightly closed.

Task at hand: Keep your mind alert to your movement and your breath. If your mind wanders off, it's ok; just recognize it and bring your attention back to your breath and your body.

Practice yoga with children

When practicing with your child, the key is to make the sessions short, fun, and varied so as to keep interest and involvement strong. With my own children, we started by practicing for about fifteen minutes at a time. This included some simple, focused breathing, a couple of animal poses, and then we would finish off with a visual relaxation. Most importantly, we experienced a peaceful time together, an awareness of our bodies, and a sense of revitalization. Begin by practicing on your own until you are comfortable with the technique. Start slow, take your time, and enjoy the feeling of being cleansed from daily stress. After you feel the peacefulness and revitalization, you then will be able to pass the benefits on to your children.

NAMASTE

—the light in you is the light in me.

"Nama" means bow, "as" means I, and
"te" means you. Therefore, Namaste,
traditionally said to one another after
yoga practice, literally means, "I bow
to the light in you." To do it: Place your
hands in prayer position resting at your
heart, with closed eyes bow connecting
to another from your divine spark,
your soul—to another.

A child's intuition

A child's body is instinctively wise to what it is capable of in regard to yoga. Ask your children to listen to their bodies, and this will guide them naturally and safely. All of my children know how to use their yoga and breathing to help their bodies relax—whether it is before bedtime, allowing a restful, peaceful night, or any time they feel the stress from the day. They learned this behavior by observing mine. Their interest in yoga began when they were little—all three of them would wander into my room, as kids do, wanting to be in the same room where I was practicing. They knew Mommy was always in a good mood when she finished her yoga. That was how it connected. It was something that struck their curiosity, it intrigued them, and of course if one of them thought it was worth trying, then they all wanted to join in. As for Sam, he learned how to help himself relax by allowing his body to move into a natural state of being and self-healing, keeping his body in balance. He now knows how to utilize this tool, using it as one part of his healthy lifestyle.

MY PRACTICE BELIEFS

- Attitude
- Attention
- Effortless asana
- Stillness
- Communion with spirit

YOGA POSTURES

Start with the basics

Begin and end every session with a short relaxation—even if it's just a few slow calming breathes to center yourself. Set the intention to shift gears and enter into a time and space dedicated to self-care.

Basics that apply to every pose

Hold the pose only as long as you feel a beautiful stretch, and you enjoy it. Listen to your body. Come out of the pose when you lose concentration, or if it begins to feel uncomfortable. Allow yourself time and attention, watch and wait for your body to respond. Remember the goal is not the glory of the pose.

SALUTE TO THE SUN

1. Mountain Pose
2. Reaching for the Sky
3. Forward Bend Pose
4. Equestrian Pose
5. Dog Pose
6. Child Pose / Kiss
7. Cobra Pose
8. Dog Pose
9. Equestrian Pose
10. Forward Bend Pose
11. Reaching for the Sky
12. Mountain Pose

Salutation to the Sun series

This graceful sequence of postures is performed in a continuous flow. It can be done quickly or slowly, but always with lots of attention to your body and your breath. The series is designed so each position is a counter pose to the previous one. It allows all of the muscles in your body to be stretched and all major organs to be stimulated. It is known as the yoga tonic. Practiced daily, this intricately designed series will give you flexibility, keep your body in good physical shape, and perhaps more importantly, help soothe your mind. It is a foundation of yoga asana.

In Salutation to the Sun both sides of your body are stretched. The second half of rounds (a round is going through the full twelve positions) consists of the same twelve positions and differs only in position four, where your right leg is taken back, and position nine, where your left foot is brought forward between the hands.

Do full rounds, stretching both sides of your body and finish with relaxation. I'll explain the poses so they can be performed as part of a series or individually.

1. Mountain Pose

This pose brings a state of concentration, calmness, and awareness to your practice. Begin by standing with your feet hip-width apart. Bring attention to your feet. Spend a few minutes letting your toes ripple on the floor. Place one toe down at a time. Feel both feet with equal amount of weight. Drop your heels into the ground. Bring your attention to your pelvis—open and wide, to your shoulders—back and down, and to your chest—open and soft. Keep your chin slightly tucked in so your neck can be long. Focus your eyes upon something in your vision at eye level. Bring attention to your breath. Watch your breath as it gently comes in and out. Feel and imitate the qualities of a mountain: grounded, still, powerful, majestic.

Mountain pose, done correctly, is the foundation of yoga postures. It is a pose to do anywhere, any time. It's a great way to give your body a break from the stresses of the day. This position helps correct your posture— it allows you to hold yourself with grace and dignity.

2. Reaching for the Sky (raised arm pose)

This pose stretches your abdominal muscles and arms, and tones your spinal cord. Begin by standing in Mountain. While inhaling slowly and deeply, allow your arms to reach up to the sky and back behind you, letting your back arch. Look up and back, keeping your neck soft and relaxed. Stretch only as far as you are comfortable; the distance will increase with practice. Exhale, then bring your arms back to the starting position.

3. Forward Bend Pose (hand to foot pose)

This is an inverted pose, meaning your head is upside down. This is great for allowing more blood to your brain, improving circulation, and it also improves digestion while keeping your spine supple. The most important thing to remember regarding this pose is that it doesn't matter how far forward your body bends.

Exhaling, bend forward from your waist until your back is flat, allowing your hands to come toward the floor, letting your head follow. It's like you're bending as a hinge from your hips. Allow your spine to lengthen. Go as far as is comfortable. If your hands do not reach the floor, use a chair or cushion to support your hands or elbows. Hold this pose only as long as you're comfortable. Bring your attention to your feet, heavy and strong on the ground. To come back up to standing, place your hands, palms together, on your chest and slowly, gently come up, one vertebra at a time. The last thing to come up is your head, as you allow your spine to follow you to standing.

4. Equestrian Pose (lunge pose)

This pose tones your abdominals and the muscles of your legs. It supplies your spinal nerves with fresh blood. Begin from a standing position. Inhale gently and slowly while moving your left leg back, into a backward stretch away from your body. Your knee can touch the floor, and your forward foot remains flat on the floor and feels heavy. Arch your back, raise your chin as you look up and allow your spine to stretch. Repeat on both sides.

5. Dog Pose

This is an all-round great pose for posture. It allows your spine to release, therefore adequately supplying blood to your spinal nerves. It is also an inverted (upside down) pose, so it gives your head a fresh supply of blood, which is great for your circulation, clearing your mind, and keeping your skin healthy.

Imagine a dog stretching its spine, yawning, hindquarters high and head low, near its paws. This is the same pose you are trying to emulate. Begin on hands and knees. Your hands and knees have become the paws of a dog. Tuck your toes under, exhale, and raise your hips toward the sky, allowing your spine movement to extend from the hips and lengthen. Your head hangs down, following your spine. Use slow and smooth focused breathing. Take care not to strain your hamstrings (the muscles at the back of your legs). Stay in this position for as long as you are comfortable.

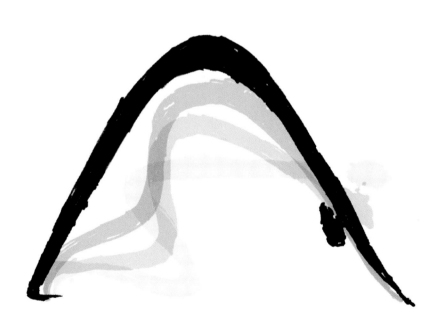

6. Child's Pose flowing into The Kiss

This posture is a wonderful stretch for your spine; it relaxes your sciatic nerve and is a good resting pose. Kneel down and sit back on your heels. Bend forward from your waist and stretch out your arms in front of you. Stretch from your hips all the way to fingers. Feel your tummy resting on your thighs, your forehead resting on the floor. Breathe in and out through your nose.

6a. The Kiss (salute with eight-limb pose)

This pose tones your shoulders and neck, developing your chest. Begin by exhaling. Lower your knees, then your chest and face, allowing your lips to "kiss the mat" as your body gently moves forward along the ground with your toes still curled under. With practice, your knees, chest, and chin will touch the floor at the same time.

7. Cobra Pose

This pose stretches your abdomen, helping with elimination or indigestion. The arching of your back exercises your spine, revitalizing important spinal nerves. It also has a balancing effect on hormones. Begin by lying on your stomach with your forehead touching the floor. Think like a snake. Make the lower part of your body heavy, just like the tail of a snake. Gently use your hands and arms to support your back and slowly lift your head. Look straight ahead, feeling strong and powerful like a cobra, ready to strike. Exhaling with a hissing sound, gently lower your body back down to the floor as in the beginning, your forehead resting on the floor.

At this point the salutation series is repeated, stretching the other side of the body. Follow the sequence with positions eight through twelve.

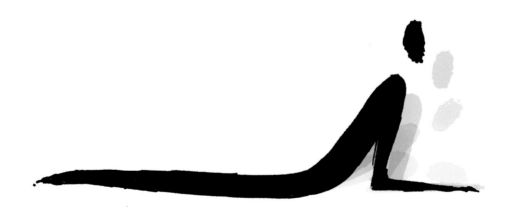

SALUTE TO THE SUN

1. Mountain Pose

2. Reaching for the Sky

3. Forward Bend Pose

4. Equestrian Pose

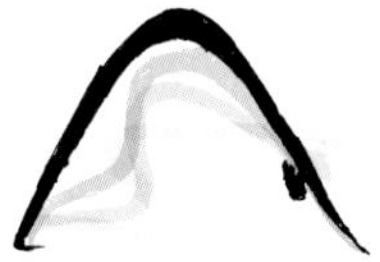

5. Dog Pose

6. Child Pose / Kiss

7. Cobra Pose

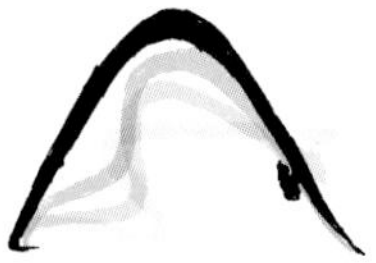

8. Dog Pose

9. Equestrian Pose

10. Forward Bend Pose

11. Reaching for the Sky

12. Mountain Pose

Tree Balance Pose

This pose develops balance and concentration. It also strengthens the muscles of your feet, ankles, and legs. Stand with your feet hip-width apart. Feel both feet equally on ground. Bring awareness to your right foot; feel its heaviness, its groundedness. Choose a spot to focus on at eye-level and keep your gaze upon it. Bring your attention to your left foot. Gently allow your left foot to rise off the floor. Feeling centered, lift your left foot and place it on the inner side of the opposite knee; raise it only as high as you feel comfortable and secure. Place your hands in prayer position on your chest. When you feel stable, raise your arms up and out like branches of a tree. Remember to keep breathing in and out through your nose. Feel your right foot, safe and grounded on the floor, as the roots of a huge tree. Imitate a tree. Feel heaviness at your base, and allow your upper body to be light and free. Soften your gaze as you continue to look straight ahead. Remain focused on your breath, and allow your body to feel still at your navel. Stay with this pose as long as it feels secure and open. Coming down, bring your arms down and your hands into prayer position at your chest. Lower your leg. Change sides and repeat. Stand with both feet on the ground, and breathe in and out.

Half Spinal Twist Pose (standing twist)

This pose helps with the flexibility of your spine and tones your spinal nerves. It also naturally massages your abdominal organs and regulates your secretion of adrenalin. Begin standing with your feet hip-width apart. Bring your awareness to your feet, heavy and grounded. Feel your feet sinking into the floor. Gently allow your arms to swing from side to side. Focus on your breath and letting go of the muscles in your lower back. Be patient—don't twist too hard. Breathe, watch, and wait for your body to respond. Feel this twisting as a very natural motion. Think heavy base, light upper body. Stay with it as long as your attention stays on your twisting.

Relaxation

The classic position of relaxation is known as Corpse Pose (lying still with no physical movement). Begin by lying down symmetrically, your head and neck in line with your spine, your shoulders rotated back and down, arms by your sides and palms face up, feet naturally turning outward. Allow your head to slowly turn side-to-side and then come back in line with spine, your chin slightly tucked in so your neck can be long, and stretch.

Sense of touch

With your eyes lightly closed, move your attention to your sense of touch. Rhythmically take your mind through the different parts of your body in contact with the ground: feet, pelvis, shoulders, and the back of your head. Feel the Earth's gravity pulling the tension from your body; allow stress and tightness to release.

Sense of hearing

Next bring your attention to sense of hearing. Listen for all sounds—loud and soft. Choose one sound and listen to only that sound, all other sounds will fade away. Allow the sound you have chosen to become loud and crystal clear.

Breathing

Bring your attention to your breath. Simply notice that you are breathing—say to yourself, "I am breathing in and I am breathing out." Breathe in and out through your nose with your mouth lightly closed, your jaw soft. Notice your inhalation and exhalation. Watch with keen attention and focus only on your breath coming in and going back out again. Feel your breath drop down deep into your belly. Hand resting on your abdomen, begin to notice the rhythm of your breathing: your hand rises on your inhalation, falls on your exhalation.

Focus your attention on the movement of your hand synchronized with the rhythm of your breathing. Stay with this practice for five minutes or more. Many physiological changes come about as your body begins to relax. Let go, and say, "ahhhh."

Take a deep breath in, and exhale. Breathe in and exhale out anything you are holding on to—any physical tightness. Breathe in and exhale out anything emotional—worries, frustrations, anger. Every time you exhale, feel your body releasing more and more.

Relax one more layer

With focused attention relax one more "layer." Begin with your toes—say to yourself, "My toes are relaxed." Follow through—feet, calves, knees, thighs, hips, back, chest, shoulders, arms, elbows, wrists, hands, fingers, neck, throat, jaw, face, and head.

Now bring your focused attention to your breath. Allow your slow, deep inhalation and even longer, deeper exhalation to soothe your body from head to toe. Become the observer of your breath. Visualize something in nature—a wave in the ocean or a branch on a tree—breathe with that movement in nature, creating stillness and quiet space.

Waking up

This practice is useful for waking up after relaxation. Wiggle your toes and fingers. Slowly breathe in and out. Stretch your arms and legs. Roll onto your side into a little ball, your chin and knees tucked into your chest. Stretch your spine; breathe in and out. Come up to a sitting position.

Body massage

Body massage feels great after a relaxation period. Rub your hands together. Generate heat within the palms of your hands and then massage your whole body—feet, legs, chest, shoulders, and head. Rub your hands together again and cup them over your eyes; feel the warmth from your hands radiating into your eyes, giving your eyes new energy. Slowly, let your hands come down and open your eyes.

BREATHING, OUR BEST FRIEND

Breath Work

Breath work traditionally follows postures as part of the complete hatha yoga practice, which includes: postures, breath work and then meditation or relaxation. However, to bring attention to your breath is something you can do anywhere, anytime—waiting in line, sitting in traffic, or before you get out of bed in the morning or fall asleep at night. Nothing acts more quickly to calm and comfort you— a built-in best friend.

A few tips to remember

With any breathing technique, there are a couple of things to remember. "Breathing normally" means breathing in and out through your nose with your mouth lightly closed. Our nose filters out impurities, adds the correct moisture, and adjusts the air to the optimal temperature for our body so that we get the best quality of air into our lungs. Knowing this—why would you want to breathe any other way?

Putting it into practice

I have chosen three of my favorite and most frequently used breathing techniques to share with you. These three methods are what I use personally and teach regularly.

Abdominal breathing

Abdominal breathing is the quickest, single thing you can do to relax your body and, therefore, your mind. I use it constantly in my private practice of teaching others how to relax.

Bring your attention to your breath. Follow your breath, and allow your mind to be the observer, watching your breath coming in and going back out. Rest your hand on your abdomen, place your thumb on your navel and let your other four fingers fan below. Feel your breath in your abdomen, and notice how your abdomen is gently rising and falling in rhythm with your breathing. As you breathe in, your abdomen rises. As you breathe out, your abdomen falls. This takes some concentration. It becomes easier with practice. Focus on your natural rhythm, smooth and effortless, breathing in and out. Let your breath soothe you, taking you to a place of comfort—the thoughts of the day disappear and life feels easier.

Add counting

Adding counting is another option when practicing abdominal breathing. It allows you to occupy both sides of your brain—right and left hemispheres. In doing this, it keeps you completely focused on your breathing. Start with the number nine and count each inhalation and exhalation as one cycle or round. Count backwards to zero. As you progress, you can increase the number. If your mind wanders off, gently bring it back and start over with your counting.

Add a mantra

Another option that helps you stay focused is adding a mantra. This time imagine there is a line that connects your navel to your throat. As you breathe in, your breath travels from your navel to your throat. As you breathe out, your breath travels from your throat to your navel. Add in the words SO-HUM. Breathing in from your navel to your throat—you say the word SO; and breathing out from your throat to your navel, you say the word HUM. In Sanskrit SO-HUM means "I am that"— beyond the limitations of body and mind, at one with the absolute.

Abdominal breathing with your child

This exercise keeps your child's total awareness on the movement of his breath. It is calming and relaxing and encourages good breathing patterns. My children prefer to keep one of their hands resting gently over their abdomen so they can feel the movement. Remind them to focus only on what you are saying and their breath. Ask your child to close his eyes and imagine a round, very soft balloon in his tummy. He can choose a color for this balloon. Ask him to breathe in slowly (always through the nose) and see the balloon gently filling up as his tummy slowly rises up towards the sky (without pushing it up). When he breathes out—the balloon empties and his tummy softly flattens. Encourage him to breathe naturally. Have him repeat this exercise five times, and ask him to notice how he feels.

Sit and breathe

Sit on your heels, cross-legged or even in a straight-backed chair. The most important thing is that you are comfortable. Feel the base of your body as being very heavy. Imagine an anchor that is thrown over the side of a boat—it is sinking and sinking until finally, it lands on the ocean floor. This anchor is like the base of your body and, as it rests on the bottom of the ocean, it feels as though it sends a ripple back up through your body, allowing your shoulders and chest to feel lighter, freer. Drop your tailbone. Drop your shoulders, and as they rotate back and down, tuck your chin in a little, and allow your neck to stretch and be long, feeling your chest open and free. It feels as though you have created more space and lightness for your upper body. Breathe in and out.

Add your arms

Inhaling, raise your arms up to the sky; exhaling, lower your arms to your sides. Repeat.

Add your arms and a hum

Inhaling, raise your arms to the sky; exhaling, make a humming sound as you lower your arms.

Bumblebee breath

In Sanskrit, mumbling breath translates to "big black bee." This "mumbling" exhalation is "cleaning" the inside of your body with the vibrations and sound. I find it extremely comforting and nurturing: a warm blanket of security. It's a wonderful remedy for relieving stress caused by anger and anxiety.

This breathing technique is done best from a sitting position. Begin by sitting on your heels or cross-legged with your spine straight. Inhale fully through your nostrils; keep your mouth soft, your teeth not touching your lips, bringing your awareness to the tiny delicate space between your lips. Exhale completely while producing a humming sound like a gentle little bumblebee. Allow the vibrations to move through your body—listen and watch your body respond to your breath. Repeat twelve times.

Opportunity is infinite

Physiologically our breath and circulatory system are linked. The air I breathe in transfers into my blood, travels around my system delivering oxygen to my brain, organs, and all other parts of my body—ending with my exhalation, which gets rid of my waste product, carbon dioxide. Then the cycle begins again.

Relationship with your breath

Besides the obvious physiological benefit of deep, full breathing cycles—learning to become more aware of your breath gives us a tool to use any time, any place. With awareness and practice, your breath becomes deeper, quieter, slower and more regular. It helps. Learning to use these simple breathing techniques begins to create a relationship between you and your breath. It is an incredible way to remove feelings of stress and anxiety, as well as encourage a relaxed, contented outlook.

Teach your child this secret

Children can feel just as "stressed out" as adults. In allowing your mind to be open to the "listening" of your inner breath, you tap into something that has always been there but now is rediscovered. By utilizing this discovery, you can give yourself a special gift that lives inside of you: a built-in defense mechanism that is always available and free to call upon whenever needed. How simple and yet deeply effective—focus on your breath. Practice on your own, get comfortable with the breathing techniques, and then pass on this gift to your child.

MEDITATION

The magic of thoughts

Thoughts are matter. However, nothing feels more magical than when your thought manifests itself into matter. Think of something. A notion created, a thought form is sent out into the atmosphere. There isn't anything magical about it. It's pure physics, the power of thought. Create what you think. Create what you believe. According to Dr. Mary Dean Atwood, author of *Spirit Healing*, a book capturing the sacred nature of Native Americans, "Native Americans realized the power of prayer, to put thoughts into words with intensity—which increases the density of the matter that makes up the thought form. This matter in turn attracts particles on the same vibratory level, continuing to build until the object is formed or materialized."

Emotions play a key role

The more emotion in my thought, the more likely it is to materialize. If I think with emotion, the process speeds up as the thought particles travel faster. Unfortunately, it can happen with negative thoughts just as quickly. Due to the emotion that I hold, the thought is strengthened or magnified. Holding confidence in my divine connection—the part of me created in the likeness of God—allows this process to unfold. Peaceful, kind, positive thoughts fueled by sincerity and love increase their speed and fruition.

This concept resonates through many religions today. The same underlying theme is repeated in different phrases: "being one with the universe," "a greater force," or "a vibrational power present in the essence of humans."

When I teach yoga, the class finishes with relaxation. This includes a moment for a positive resolve or a prayer for a helpful change in the student's life. When the mind and body are relaxed and in a receptive state, thoughts become increasingly powerful. I always remind my students to choose their positive statement carefully, as a seed planted in fertile ground grows swiftly and beautifully.

Uncover the goodness within

The Blue Mountain Center for Meditation was established in 1961 at UC Berkeley by Eknath Easwaran, an Indian professor who came to the U.S. on a Fulbright scholarship in 1959. One of my favorite authors on meditation, Easwaran eloquently describes meditation this way: "Love, compassion, meaning, hope, and freedom from fear are not qualities we need to acquire. We simply need to uncover what we already have." For decades he taught his eight-point program for meditation, the basic principles of which are more than the time I spend "eyes closed" in meditation. It also incorporates the following practices into my life: using a mantra (of my choice) throughout the day, generally slowing down and simplifying life, training my attention to the task at hand (no more multi-tasking), training my senses (choosing carefully what I eat, read, watch, and listen to), developing an innate concern for other people's welfare, cultivating spiritual companionship (spending time with people whose company promotes my growth), and reading spiritual literature every day. You, and your children, can benefit just as much from this practice as I do.

PRESENT MOMENT

"I have no time to meditate"

Any time can be meditation time. Simple everyday activities become an avenue for creating quiet space in my mind. Whether I fold laundry, wash a dish, or lead a meeting—if I use focused attention, acknowledge wandering thoughts, and bring my attention back to the task at hand—I am meditating. Tasks throughout the day, previously what may have seemed "time wasters," now done with a single, calm concentration, become a meditation incorporated into my daily routine. Keep a relaxed and alert attention during the day, and "mindless" chores become "mindful."

Meditation helps my mind become quiet and still—my brain of constant thoughts craves silent space. Dedicating effort to this practice is worth every minute—the payback is an open and clear inner space allowing a reflection of my true self. Learning to meditate in only a small way can help so much. It gives me tranquility, energy, clarity, and security—tools for life and worth every second invested.

In the rush of modern life, we tend to lose touch with the peace that is available in each moment. The most profound satisfactions, the deepest feelings of joy and completeness lie as close at hand as our next aware breath and the smile we can form right now.

— Thich Nhat Hanh, Zen master, peace activist, and author

How to get started

The ritual of a routine is the key to success with any practice. Discipline, determination, and designating a regular time each day create a rhythm. Following is a specific meditation practice from the Bihar School of Yoga in Munger, India, known as "Inner Silence." It is an invaluable practice that is now a life skill for me—a means to help me relax and unlock the gift of self-awareness.

Let's relax and practice Inner Silence

Sense of touch

Get comfortable. Lie down symmetrically, your head and neck in line with your spine. Allow your legs to turn out with your feet naturally turning outward. Place your arms down by your sides and let your palms face up, your shoulders rotating back and down into the ground. Allow your head to turn slowly side to side and then come in line with your spine, your chin slightly tucked in so your neck can be long, and stretch. Close your eyes and focus your attention on the exterior—your sense of touch. Take your mind rhythmically through the different parts of your body that are touching the mat: your feet, pelvis, shoulders, and the back of your head. Feel Earth's gravity pulling the tension from your body, allowing your body to release tension and tightness. Stay with this practice of "feeling" for a few minutes.

Awareness to sense of hearing

Next bring your attention to your sense of hearing. Listen for all the sounds you can hear. Listen for loud sounds and soft sounds. After spending a few minutes with this, choose one sound and listen to only that sound, excluding all others.

Awareness to your breath

Now bring your awareness to your breath. Just simply notice that you are breathing. Simply notice your breath. You can say to yourself, "I am breathing in and I am breathing out." Breathe in and out through your nose. Notice your inhalation and your exhalation—feel your breath drop into

Be gentle on yourself.

Try relaxing for five minutes in the morning before you get out of bed, and five minutes in the evening before you go to sleep. Notice how you feel after you relax. Soon your body will crave this feeling, and your practice will become a welcomed habit in your day.

your abdomen. Feel your abdomen slowly and gently rising and falling with the rhythm of your breathing—soft and natural. Watch with keen attention, focusing only on your breath coming in and then your breath going back out again. Stay with this practice for a while. Notice any thoughts coming into your mind. You are the observer watching your thoughts. Now focus your attention back on your breath. Continue with this practice for a while, back and forth—watching your thoughts and then back to watching your breath. You are becoming more still and quiet. Stay with this for a while as your body is becoming closer to it's natural state and is healed and renewed.

Begin with five minutes practice a day. Stay with this practice for five minutes and then gradually add in five minutes more until you reach your goal of twenty. Many physiological changes take place as your body begins to relax. Begin to notice how you feel after you relax.

When the mind is silent and peaceful, it becomes very powerful. It becomes the receptor of bliss and wisdom, and life becomes a spontaneous flow and expression of joy. All this arises naturally when the mind is in an inner state of silence.

—Swami Satyananda Saraswati

Teaching relaxation to children

Meditation is an invaluable skill for adults. Imagine what a gift it is for our children! Teaching children to relax is laying the groundwork for later years of meditation, and this very simple and practical way gives them a key. The key opens a door to self-understanding, confidence, and peace. Empowering them with this knowledge creates a priceless gift from you. They learn through your example, watching and absorbing. Teach them how to meditate in a very simple way. It gives them an avenue to create a better life for themselves and learn how to cope and adjust to the demanding pace of this generation.

Daytime relaxation

Teach your child this simple skill, and she will reap the benefits for her lifetime. Begin with the "inner silence" method above to relax. Next step, create color, waves, and a memory with your child.

Add color

Ask your child to think about a color. Tell her to use the color that comes to mind. To imagine breathing in the color, to feel the color filling her body. Exhale and see the color fade away.

Add waves

Now ask your child to see a wave in the ocean. Tell her to imagine her breath is like a wave in the ocean—feel her breath just like the wave, watching the wave like her breath come in and go out again. Talk to your kids about breathing with the waves, to count them, see them, and smell them. Try to practice for five minutes every day, increasing to more time, as it gets easier.

Watch and notice

Ask your child how she feels after the relaxation. If she feels good, ask her to make a memory of it. Tell her to carry this feeling with her "in her pocket" and to remember she can pull out this feeling and use it anytime she wants to feel good.

Bedtime meditation

Take a journey in the imagination. It is a simple way to begin building the foundation of meditation with children. This experience gives kids a chance to unwind and to begin to relax. Set aside a little time before bed and give your kids a great reason to put off "lights out" a little longer!

Using imagination through visualization

Visualization is a beautiful way to re-live the ancient tradition of storytelling. Here are a few ideas to spark your own creativity. Through the years my children and I have enjoyed many different shared journeys in our imaginations, giving them a place to be anywhere and do anything they want. Empowering them with this tool reminds them how to dig into their creative minds. It gives them the opportunity to use this instinctive nature that children have, however sometimes forgotten in our fast-paced society. And, who knows? Perhaps one day your child will pass it on to the next generation.

Always begin with a relaxation

Begin with the "inner silence" method above to relax. Next step, try out one of the three following visualizations.

SEEING A STAR

A bright, clear spacious sky filled with twinkling stars. Find your star. See it above your head. It is very special, as it is your very own star. No one else has one like it. Choose a color for your star. Your star is filled with your color, which is now glowing and shimmering. See the light coming down from your star and coming into your head. Feel this pure, sparkling light fill your body. It fills you from the top of your head, down your arms, into your fingers, tummy, legs and right down to your toes. Look into your heart and fill it with love for all the people and animals you know (adapt to your situation). Remember they are friends. Do you feel love that is in your heart? Can you feel it getting bigger? It is getting bigger because you have so much love in your heart for all these people and animals, and of course for you.

Look back to the clear sky. Find your special star. Make a wish on this star and send this prayer across the sky. Know in your heart, your intention and purpose are of the highest honor, confident your star's journey into the cosmos will benefit goodness and light.

THE RAINBOW

Walk down a winding, cobblestone pathway. Notice green bushes and little delicate white flowers sprouting up on either side. A handsome wooden bench made from a tree trunk sits beside the pathway. It looks so comfortable to sit down and take a rest. Across the pathway a silent, still pond lies ahead in this peaceful woodland setting. Look closely and see the pond's surface has small tiny droplets—it's beginning to gently rain. The large oak tree spreads its branches to protect you and keeps the rain away. The rain smells fresh and pure, a natural clean feeling.

The rain begins to stop as the sun peeks out from behind the clearing. Sunshine streams through the trees like rays from heaven, reflections of glimmering colored lights. A rainbow forms. Looking at each color of the rainbow, breathe in the colors one at a time. Red; breathe in the color red. Exhale as it fades away. Orange; breathe in the color orange. Exhale as it fades away. Yellow; breathe in the color yellow. Exhale as it fades away. Green; breathe in the color green. Exhale as it fades away. Blue; breathe in the color blue. Exhale as it fades away. Purple; breathe in the color purple. Exhale as it fades away. Look closely at the end of the rainbow. A pile of gold is shimmering in the sunshine. It feels like all the love and goodness in the world. See the color gold; breathe in the color gold. Exhale as it fades away. Think of a favorite color. Breathe in this color, soothing and cleansing. Exhale as it fades away. Refreshed and renewed, follow the steps back down the path, knowing you can come back to this special place any time.

SOARING WITH THE EAGLE

Lying on warm, green grass, feel its gentle softness. See a crystal blue sky—your thoughts are like white clouds passing by. In the distance a magnificent eagle is soaring, graceful and free. He extends an invitation to take wing with him and soar through the sky. Floating down, he sits on the ground. His back is soft. He feels safe, like being in a gigantic feather bed. Climbing in the air, you feel so free. A village below comes to view. Deerskin teepees with clouds of smoke swirling up and out of their tops create a welcoming place. Water splashes on stones in the clear, crisp river next to the village. Indian women collect water as their children play and laugh in the shallow water. Majestic snow-topped mountains circle the village, creating a sense of protection from the outside world. Eagle friend flies so effortlessly, floating through the air and you are filled with peace. The sun creates a warm feeling of comfort in the cool sky. Enjoy this magical scene. Take a minute to be in this peaceful, free, safe place. Eagle friend gently maneuvered his way safely back down to the ground. Come back to the soft, green, warm grass. Climb off his back, grateful for and rested from this journey, sitting down on the warm earth.

So much fun

Visualizations are so much fun. Use these examples to get started tapping into the creative mind with your child. Take turns. Let your child guide you in a journey. The enjoyment is being creative and spending relaxing special time together. Plus the benefit in teaching your child a tool to relax, renew and feel good about themselves.

A gift for their lifetime

What greater gift can we give our children than the gift of inner peace? My children's bedtime became a time to relax, be together and have some fun being creative. It became a very straightforward and natural way to give them a gift for the remainder of their lives. This gift leads us to a world of calmly confident and centered adults, creating a brighter future for us all.

VISUALIZE WITH YOUR CHILD

Visualization is a beautiful way to re-live the ancient tradition of storytelling. Through the years my children and I have enjoyed many different shared journeys in our imaginations, giving them a place to be anywhere and do anything they want. Empowering them with this tool reminds them how to dig into their creative minds. It gives them the opportunity to use this instinctive nature that children have sometimes forgotten in our fast-paced society.

Chapter 3: Yoga : Breathing, Body Awareness and Meditation

Q: *Yoga is so popular now. Is it any different than any other kind of exercise class?*

A: When I shifted into practicing yoga everyday in my own home instead of a few times a week with a class I noticed a clear transition in my life. For me, yoga is much more than the exercise time spent on my mat. It is about living my yoga, which means incorporating the principles in this chapter into my everyday life and experiences. The true essence of this practice—the bringing together of body and mind, connects me to my divine spark and lets me flow in the spirit of God. It is then that I am truly practicing yoga.

Q: *I have a full-time job, three kids, two dogs and a husband who works all the time. Do you really think I can feel calm and balanced with all of this going on?*

A: I am so passionate about this process of teaching others how to bring their body into balance. Believe me, I was not always this way. Through my son's birth and then dealing with his illness, I was pushed into a healthier lifestyle which was the beginning for me of understanding the true nature, the depths of my body's ability to perform when allowed to do what it is capable of. Within the next year I became involved with yoga. Yoga helped me understand more fully how to use breathing and body awareness and relaxation to open up to the intrinsic nature of my own body more often. I began to see the shifts in what was happening to me and got very excited to share that information and experience with others because I know it is possible. Everyone has the capability—it's just about opening up to the opportunity. This ability is innate. I give you the guidelines in this book, but the destination is always found on our own.

Q: *What about meditation? I have tried "meditating" but always get frustrated. I can't seem to relax and focus even for a few minutes. What can you suggest?*

A: Be gentle on yourself. Your practice may be as simple as doing the guided relaxation "inner silence" I describe in this chapter for five minutes in the morning before you get out of bed, and five minutes in the evening before you go to sleep. Many physiological changes take place as your body begins to relax. Begin to notice how you feel after you relax. This time will soon become a welcomed habit.

Q: *Why do I want to teach my children about these practices?*

A: Teaching children to relax their body and mind is laying the groundwork for later years of meditation, and the practical ways described in this chapter gives them that key. The key opens a door to self-understanding, confidence, and peace. Teach them some of these techniques in a very simple way. It gives them an avenue to create a better life for themselves and learn how to cope and adjust to the demanding pace of this generation.

4

Alternative Therapies Explained

The doctor of the future will give no medicine,
but will interest his patients in the care of the human
frame, in diet, and in the cause and prevention of disease.
—THOMAS EDISON

In my speaking engagements and workshops I teach mothers methods to create balance and well-being in their daily life. I emphasize that it is never one thing that brings us to a physical or emotional unhealthy state—but a million little things that add up. And so, we cannot expect one thing to create a new healthy way of being. It is instead the combination of practices—gentle yoga, breathing and relaxation techniques, mindful awareness in everyday life, enjoying what you do, solid habits of good nutrition—that brings a natural way of being from the inside out. This combination of ideas also forms a preventive plan that remains true to the most basic doctrine of medical law: "First, do no harm."

For my family and me, complementary practices—ways to wellbeing that fall outside the scope of Western medicine—work to help us keep our healthy lifestyle. What follows is a simplistic overview of my personal favorite complementary practices—Ayurveda, homeopathy, acupuncture, and bodywork. I believe these practices help us help our bodies to self-heal and form the foundation of centuries of medicine.

My family is not alone in employing these remedies. NCCAM (The National Center for Complementary and Alternative Medicine) says Americans fork out 34 billion dollars annually for complementary and alternative medicine. According to *Time Magazine,* three-quarters of U.S.

medical schools offer courses in the subject. People are catching this holistic wave coming through America, a wave that other societies have embraced for centuries, as we look for alternative therapies that work. All of the holistic approaches to follow offer a new dimension of hope through the emphasis on prevention, something that can bring much needed relief to a nation in the midst of a health care crisis.

AYURVEDA

What is Ayurveda?

Simply put, the words means "balance of life." In Sanskrit (the sacred language of India and yoga),

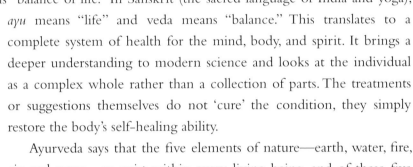

ayu means "life" and veda means "balance." This translates to a complete system of health for the mind, body, and spirit. It brings a deeper understanding to modern science and looks at the individual as a complex whole rather than a collection of parts. The treatments or suggestions themselves do not 'cure' the condition, they simply restore the body's self-healing ability.

Ayurveda says that the five elements of nature—earth, water, fire, air, and space—co-exist within every living being, and of these five elements, three predominate. This is what makes up a person's dosha *(dah-sha)*.

Why do we care?

Understanding this philosophy can bring self-awareness; when we don't see a habit or issue within us, it is difficult to change. And, of course, being able to pass this understanding on to our children gives them a tool for their lifetime.

For me, the easiest way to understand any concept is to see a real-life example. Following are three descriptions of the various characteristics representing the three different doshas governing health and energy. It is important to understand that each person holds all three doshas, with one being dominant.

The three doshas

Kapha *(principal of structure)*

Starting from the ground up, with the Earth element, keeps it easy. My girlfriend is a typical kapha. She has a large, solid body frame and is slow and steady, mellow; she never forgets things and is incredibly grounded, as you would think of an Earth element. Blessed with a sweet, affectionate nature, she loves to hug. She is known to many as a "Mother Earth." Kaphas typically are lethargic and tend to struggle with weight gain. Our personalities go well together. We balance each other. She is calming kapha, and I am quick-moving, energetic vata. Basic steps, such as picking up the pace with a brisk walk, increasing her digestive fire with ginger tea or spicy foods, or varying the daily routine, help keep her in balance. Can you think of a mother or child that you know who holds kapha as their predominate dosha? Children who struggle with weight gain are often kapha types. If you understand this about your child at an early age, you can help them offset their sluggish tendencies and bring more balancing activities and foods into their life early on, creating healthy habits when they are most needed.

Pita *(transformation)*

Next comes the pita dosha. My husband comes first to my mind as a classic pita. He is analytical, driven, and intense, with an incredible work ethic. He has a medium frame, eyes that take in everything, and you can tell he is always thinking, analyzing, and processing. Like many pitas, he is good with numbers and has a head for business. He is quick to anger, but also generously forgiving and honest. He sets boundaries for work, and uses music or a cooling swim as a means of balancing his fire. Avoiding hot and spicy foods, especially in the summer months, also keeps him in balance. Children with classic pita doshas need help with calming techniques. A bedtime routine that includes breathing and counting, combined with a guided visualization, can really help them "turn off" their ever-working mind and get some much need rest.

Vata *(air)*

The third dosha is vata, of which I am a fairly classic example…I am known to flit from one thing to another, quick thinking, with lots of energy and creativity. I am intuitive, with a slender body frame. I tend to take ideas in quickly, but can have trouble remembering them. Yoga is an important tool to quiet, center, and ground myself. Warm, calming foods and soothing herbal teas keep me in equilibrium. Now that I know these techniques, whenever I am starting to feel out of balance I know what to do. Children with a vata constitution love a routine. An established meal and bedtime creates predictable security that we crave, helping us stay in balance.

Self care

In the belief system of Ayurveda we all are multilayered beings influenced by our diet, emotions, and environment. Above all, Ayurveda is a system of self-care. Listen to your body. What is it trying to tell you? What are your symptoms speaking to you about? Don't mask these important clues. Instead use them to understand the root of a problem. Learn to be aware of who you are in relationship to your environment. These ideas allow an awareness that self-monitors your body, keeping you healthy and happy. My goal is to help mothers and children come from a centered place somewhere deep inside—maybe best described as true beauty flowing from inner to outer.

In a nutshell

"According to Ayurvedic principles, by understanding oneself, by identifying one's own constitution, and by recognizing sources of doshic aggravation, one can not only follow the proper guidelines to cleanse, purify, and prevent disease, but also uplift oneself into a realm of awareness previously unknown."
—Vasant Lad, MASc, Ayurvedic physician and director of the Ayurvedic Institute in
Albuquerque, New Mexico

Ayurveda says that every person is unique, and the importance of self-understanding is the ultimate goal, the foundation of life. To understand myself in regards to my dosha, I can better understand what makes up my psychological and physical strengths and weaknesses. In this way I can anticipate illness or imbalances and take precautions to avoid them—altering my routine, diet, exercise, or environment. With perseverance and practice, I allow my body to move into a natural rhythm of health and wellbeing.

Paying attention to the seasons—respectful of each season for its beauty and its natural rhythm of sleep and wakefulness—is an example of Ayurveda's essence in bringing balance into my life. Reverence to the time of year reflects my own innate relationship, keeping me aware and sensitive to the ever-changing cycle of life. The principles of Ayurveda help bring equilibrium to my life, but it isn't always easy. When I have an aching head, feel scattered and overwhelmed, I now step back and take a wider view. Sometimes using humor, surrendering to the situation, or feeling compassion for another brings me back in touch with the here and now. It may be a simple awareness to the present moment, or grounding myself through breathing and body awareness and meditation, or eating a vata-calming diet. A combination of these practices acts as a remedy, which allows me to move with the ebb and flow, maintaining a vibrant equilibrium in my dance with life.

> The body must be credited with an immense fund of know-how. The first question an Ayurvedic physician asks is not 'What disease does my patient have?' but 'Who is my patient?' By 'who,' the physician does not mean your name, but how you are constituted.
> —Deepak Chopra, M.D
>
> When diet is wrong medicine is of no use. When diet is correct medicine is of no need.
> —Ayurvedic proverb

HOMEOPATHY

> The highest ideal of cure is the speedy, gentle, and enduring restoration of health by the most trustworthy and least harmful way.
> —Samuel Hahnemann, founder of homeopathy

My first experience with homeopathy was almost twenty years ago, walking into the chemist's shop off a busy street in London. Intrigued by the beautifully organized rows of tiny blue bottles along the shelf, my curiosity led me to ask the shopkeeper what they were. He replied that they were homeopathic remedies.

Homeopathy is used by hundreds of millions of people worldwide and is derived from the Greek words homios meaning "similar" and pathos meaning "suffering." Homeopathy works on the basic principle of "like cures like." The remedies taken are derived from plants, minerals, and animals, and are dispensed in tiny bottles of elixir. The remedy's job is to match the symptom pattern of illness, which in turn stimulates the body's natural healing response.

Living in England, we adopted this therapy as part of our family's approach in caring for the common cold, allergies, or emotional upsets, even as a jet-lag remedy. Our family physician, an M.D. who practiced homeopathy, educated us over the years, and as I saw results, we experienced what this two hundred-year-old system of medicine had to offer. In Britain, entire hospitals and clinics are dedicated exclusively to its practice. Not only is it part of Britain's National Health System, six generations of the royal family used this type of medicine.

COMMON HOMEOPATHIC REMEDIES

Here are a few common homeopathic remedies to give you a glimpse of their curative powers.

- **Arnica** is commonly used in creams for bruises, muscle sprains, and soreness. It is made from the fresh flowering plant in the mountains of Europe known as "mountain tobacco," where mountain climbers chewed the fresh plant to relieve sore, aching muscles.

- **Sulphur** is a mineral found in every cell of the body. A fine yellow powder extracted from the mineral, which is found near volcanic craters in Italy and the United States. It is commonly known to treat skin conditions, such as eczema and thrush.

- **Pulsatilla,** a delicate plant with a long history of medicinal uses, comes from the Pasque, or wind flower, that is native to Scandinavia, Germany, and Russia. In homoeopathy it has a wide range of uses, most commonly for colds and coughs.

- **Ignatia** seeds from the native East Indies tree create a remedy used to treat emotional problems. It is named after Ignatius Loyola, who was a Catholic priest and founder of the Jesuit order.

> Opposites are cures for opposites.
>
> —HIPPOCRATES

Homeopathy's history

In the 1800s, German doctor and chemist Samuel Hahnemann didn't agree with the harsh treatments of this time, which included blood-letting and drastic doses of medicine that produced terrible side effects. He was a great believer in the curative powers of a healthy diet and body hygiene. After many years of dedicated study and research, Hahnemann made the breakthrough, coming to the conclusion that when the remedies were diluted, they were paradoxically greater in strength. Hahnemann's discoveries led to a new system of medicine based on the idea that a drug in small amounts will cure the same symptoms it causes in large amounts—homeopathy.

In 1849, the first homeopathic hospital was built in London; the death rate from cholera at that hospital was 30 percent lower than in other hospitals. In the early 1900s, Dr. Tyler Kent, an American doctor and homeopath, studied how different kinds of people reacted to certain remedies more effectively than others. He founded the idea that people with similar body shapes and personalities tend to have similar diseases. This valuable information is now used along with the symptoms when diagnosing illness and prescribing remedies, a part of classic homeopathy. Recent numerous, scientific, double-blind studies published in prestigious journals, such as the *Lancet* and the *British Journal of Clinical Pharmacology,* prove the effectiveness of homeopathic remedies, and more and more people continue to take notice of this type of treatment.

Vital force

Homeopathic remedy's potency is this: The more diluted the remedy, the greater its potency. Hahnemann believed there must be subtle energy within the body, which responded to this tiny aggravation when the remedy was taken, allowing the body to heal itself. The explanation of homeopathic remedies appears to lie in the domain of quantum physics and the emerging field of energy medicine. And, the main reason homeopathy is viewed with skepticism by many orthodox medical practices is the dilution of the original substance.

To wrap it up

Unlike pharmaceuticals, homeopathic remedies come from inexpensive natural substances—unable to patent—so no drug company will provide funds for research to gain FDA approval as with conventional drugs. However, the World Health Organization cites homeopathy as one of the systems of traditional medicine that should be integrated worldwide with conventional medicine in order to provide adequate global health in the twenty-first century. As the pendulum swings in this generation's eagerness for knowledge about alternative medicine, the popularity of this gentle system —allowing health and healing in an effective and least harmful way—is sure to find its place.

WHO USES HOMEOPATHIC REMEDIES?

- Every pharmacy in Germany and France stocks homeopathic remedies.
- It is the most popular type of cold and flu medicine in France.
- It is the most popular hay fever remedy in Germany.
- Mother Teresa had a special interest in homeopathy because of its effectiveness and low cost in 1950 in Calcutta.
- In 2009, Americans spent three billion dollars on homeopathic medicine.

The concepts of disease and healing which are described in homeopathic books are quite similar to modern scientific concepts. Homeopathy emphasizes the importance of treating individuals as individuals and of understanding the whole person as opposed to only understanding a single diseased part.

—British Homeopathic Association

ALTERNATIVE THERAPIES EXPLAINED

ACUPUNCTURE

I remember Sam's first visit to an acupuncturist. It was late autumn, the time of year when the constant sound of coughing, sneezing, and throat-clearing surrounded us. Unfortunately, Sam picked up a virus and entered into a full-blown cycle of I-can't-breathe misery. A trip to our nearby pediatrician confirmed there was no bacterial infection, so we headed off to see the acupuncturist. Driving closer to Chinatown, Sam noticed the Asian street signs. He and I both felt a nervous excitement as we were on an adventure; we weren't just driving across town, we were entering a different world.

The acupuncturist's warm and welcome hello instantly put Sam at ease. He told Sam that acupuncture may initially feel like a mosquito bite; it may sting, but then it goes away. The acupuncturist then carefully placed twelve, single-use, extremely thin sterile needles at strategic points, three being directly around the nose and sinus cavity. Only seven years old, Sam handled it like a true man. Almost immediately he could breathe clearly. As he took in some long, deep breaths from both nostrils, a huge smile broadened across his face and he said, "It feels good to breathe."

How does acupuncture work?

Acupuncture originated in China thousands of years ago, and is now the most widely used integrative therapy in the U.S. The Chinese believe health comes from harmonious balance between the complementary extremes—yin and yang, which is the life force known as *qui* (pronounced chee). That qui flows through pathways (meridians) in your body, which are accessible through acupuncture points. Stimulating these points corrects the imbalance of energy flow and rebalances the body.

Yin, yang, and the seasons

The Chinese also use the five elements—water, wood, fire, earth, and metal—to classify the organs and tissues. These five elements need to be working in harmony with respect to seasonal changes in order for yin and yang to be in balance.

To understand this philosophy better, I like to use the example of a seed planted in the spring that then blooms into a flower in the summer, seeds itself in autumn, and dies back in winter, with a new cycle beginning again the next spring. This creates a never-ending cycle with each season playing its role. The same process happens within our body—cells grow and die, and our body's systems work together in harmony with the seasons in a similar way to ensure balance of body, mind, spirit and the healthy flow of life. Interesting, that within my personal experience of helping others find health and well being, the time of seasonal change tends to be an increased time of illness. This anecdotal evidence seems to support the belief that a combination of several factors contributes to the imbalance of our "mini universe," making us more vulnerable to disease and illness at these times. Overeating causes our body to work overtime, filtering toxins and producing heat from the excess food and drink. Add in a fast-paced lifestyle and top it off with a seasonal change, and it all adds up to imbalance.

Does it always work?

Misdiagnosis and misplacement of the needles are probably the biggest reason acupuncture doesn't work. It's impossible to balance organs in treating an underlying disease if the practitioner makes the wrong diagnosis. In addition, the exact points are not anatomical, so the point can slightly shift. If the correct spot isn't used, no real benefit is gained.

Choosing an acupuncture practitioner

My first step in finding either a conventional or complementary doctor or practitioner is personal recommendation. Ask someone you trust for recommendations. Next, check out the practitioner's training and credentials. I always suggest using someone who has been practicing acupuncture for a long time—as in any craft, experience combined with knowledge creates wisdom.

> It's impossible to balance organs in treating an underlying disease if the practitioner makes the wrong diagnosis.

Bodywork, a world of touch

I could be described as a tactile person. I enjoy making physical contact with others, and most of the time others feel the same. Okay, around my house I am known as a "hugger," I just love to give a big mama bear hug as family and friends come and go. Whenever my kids introduce me to their friends, I instantly move towards them and wrap them in a friendly hug. Quickly assuring their friends my kids say, "Don't worry. My mom is a hugger. She can't help it."

Touch me gently

Even if you're not a hugger like I am, I'm sure you can appreciate how it feels to have your arm or cheek caressed by a baby, or even to have your head massaged when being shampooed before a haircut. In my nursing experience, I remember the importance of cuddling babies, as the positive effects of touch and healing are scientifically linked in numerous studies. Touch is an essential form of human communication. It's unnatural to suppress it. A recent *Wall Street Journal* article said, "even online we have found a way to evoke touch: Witness the Facebook 'poke' and Twitter's 'nudge.'" Here's a little fact about our sense of touch: Human skin is our body's largest organ. It serves us as an amazing protective, physical barrier. It also, with some four million sensory receptors, is highly responsive to the sense of touch. With even a little brush or gentle pat, our sensory receptors send a message directly to our brains—saying "oh-laa-laa," it feels good to be touched!

Invest in YOU

As a mom, especially if you have young kids, you might feel like you're touched too much—with some little person always tugging on your sleeve, asking to be picked up. But the truth is that investing in regular 'maintenance' bodywork exposes you to a very different kind of touch and will reward you in numerous dividends. A bonus of any bodywork therapy is a feeling of indulgence. But more than that, it's a powerful preventive health investment. Bodywork helps relieve the stress and tension that our body builds up from its day-to-day wear and tear. This collective "build-up" can lead to disease and illness. Bodywork feels good; it reduces stress and fatigue, improves circulation as well as taps into our natural reservoir of energy system, awakening our own self-healing capacity.

What is Bodywork?

Here are a few of my favorite types of bodywork (with terms and definitions) to lighten the load.

Bodywork Therapies: different therapies using various forms of touch, movement, manipulation or "re-patterning" to effect a structural change.

Massage is a type of bodywork with roots dating back some three thousand years. This ancient ritual is much more than a luxurious hour spent at the spa. It stimulates sensory receptors that relax body (and therefore mind)—a perfect preventive health elixir. Many of us—39 million in all, that's one in six Americans—have had at least one massage according to a national survey by American Massage Therapy Association.

Rolfing is a method of bodywork developed by Pauline Rolf with the goal of organizing our human structure in relation to gravity. It involves manipulating our body's connective tissues in order to release stress patterns. Previously known as "structural integration" it weighs in as a great way to "undo" built-up body stresses and move into a lighter, easier place.

Chiropractic system is based on the concept that the nervous system coordinates all of our body's functions. One main goal of this work is to relieve pressure on nerves coming from the spinal cord that may be displaced. This can be done with an "activator" or a physical manual adjustment. Many chiropractors use a combination of muscle-relaxing methods to relieve our stressed-out bodies in relationship to our spine.

Craniosacral therapy is a gentle, hands-on approach that releases tensions deep in the body to improve whole-body health. Using a soft touch—about five grams of pressure, the weight of a nickel—practitioners release restrictions in the soft tissue that surround the central nervous system.

IDEAS TO KEEP IN MIND WHEN INVESTING TIME AND MONEY IN BODYWORK THERAPY

- **Take a warm shower and stretch** (or do some yoga) before you go. Make the effort to prepare for your treatment session. It's worth it. Racing in to your appointment feeling completely stressed-out can minimize your benefit. If you've done a little "prep" work (being more relaxed and loosened up in general), it can allow your therapist to begin working on you from an easier place and add to your overall benefit.

- **Drink plenty of water before and after your session.** Toxins can be released during your treatment and water helps flush them out.

- **How to find a good practitioner?** Ask around. Personal recommendation is always best. If that's not an option, see the resource section at the back of this book.

> Homeopathy cures a greater percentage of cases than any other method of treatment.
> It is the latest refined method of treating patients economically and non-violently.
> — Gandhi

Self-massage can be a beautiful option

Following are a couple of my favorite self-massages. Even better, get your kid, partner, or a friend to do a "trade" with you! Take a moment and indulge yourself right now.

UNTIE THE KNOTS IN YOUR NECK

- **Place your hands over your shoulders.** Breathing out, slowly allow your head to gently drop back as you squeeze your fingers towards your palms, inching your way up your shoulders towards your neck.

- **Now place your hands on the back of your head** and interlace your fingers. Breathing out, slowly drop your head forward as you allow the weight of your elbows to pull your head gently down, stretching out the muscles of your neck and back.

SOOTHE YOUR TIRED FEET

- **Sitting in a chair,** hold your left foot so you can see the sole of your foot. Starting at the heel apply firm pressure with your right thumb, working up the "spine" of your foot to your big toe.

- **Now walk your thumb across** the ball of your foot.

- **When you reach your little toe,** use your thumb and index finger to squeeze, gently twist and pull the entire surface of each toe. Working with each toe until you reach your big toe.

- **Support the top of your left foot** with your left hand. Use your right hand's knuckles and apply deep pressure to the entire surface of your foot. Start at your heel and work to your toes and then back down again.

- **Finally, stretch out your toes,** flex and extend your feet, and rotate your ankles a few times.

- **Repeat** the entire process on your right foot.

One final thought: Whatever practices you choose to help keep you in balance, **your body is the greatest instrument you will ever own. Take good care of it.**

Chapter 4: Alternative Therapies Explained

Q: *I feel overwhelmed and stressed-out by my life. I don't know where to start in trying to get healthy, what do you suggest I do?*

A: I emphasize that it is never one thing that brings us to a physical or emotional unhealthy state—but a million little things that add up. And so, we cannot expect one thing to create a new healthy way of being. It is instead the combination of practices—gentle yoga, breathing and relaxation techniques, mindful awareness in everyday life, enjoying what you do, solid habits of good nutrition—that brings a natural way of being from the inside out. This combination of ideas also forms a preventive plan that remains true to the most basic doctrine of medical law: "First, do no harm."

Q: *What is Ayurveda? Can you help me understand more about this approach? How can it help me?*

A: In the belief system of Ayurveda we all are multilayered beings influenced by our diet, emotions, and environment. Ayurveda is a system of self-care. Listen to your body. What is it trying to tell you? What are your symptoms speaking to you about? Don't mask these important clues. Instead use them to understand the root of a problem. Learn to be aware of who you are in relationship to your environment. These ideas allow an awareness that self-monitors your body, keeping you healthy and happy. My goal is to help mothers and children come from a centered place somewhere deep inside—maybe best described as true beauty flowing from inner to outer.

Q: *How did you come to know about homeopathy? How can this practice help my family, and can I trust this concept?*

A: Living in England, we adopted this therapy as part of our family's approach in caring for the common cold, allergies, or emotional upsets, even as a jet-lag remedy. Our family physician, an MD who practiced homeopathy, educated us over the years, and as I saw results we experienced what this two hundred–year-old system of medicine had to offer. In Britain, entire hospitals and clinics are dedicated exclusively to its practice. Not only is it part of Britain's National Health System, six generations of the royal family used this type of medicine.

Q: *Can you explain the basic concept of Chinese medicine, specifically, acupuncture?*

A: Think of the four seasons and the neverending cycle, with each season playing its role. The same process happens within our body—cells grow and die, and our body's systems work together in harmony with the seasons in a similar way to ensure balance of body, mind, spirit and the healthy flow of life. Acupuncture works in creating a harmonious balance between the complementary extremes—yin and yang, the life force known as *qui* (pronounced "chee").

Q: *I would love to treat myself to a massage on a regular basis, but it feels so indulgent and I feel guilty for spending the time and money on myself. What do you think?*

A: A bonus of any bodywork therapy is a feeling of indulgence. But more than that, it's a powerful preventative health investment. Bodywork helps relieve the stress and tension that our body builds up from its day-to-day wear and tear. This collective "build-up" can lead to disease and illness. Bodywork feels good because it reduces stress and fatigue, improves circulation, and taps into our natural energy reservoir, awakening our own self-healing capacity. Please don't feel guilty. Your positive health ripples out to everyone you come in contact with—and that's time and money well spent.

ALTERNATIVE THERAPIES EXPLAINED

5

The Big Three: Difficult Challenges for Today's Kids

Dealing with stress and its myriad repercussions is the number one issue I am asked to respond to when helping mothers and children. That is why I have dedicated much of this book to how to reduce stress for you and your family. Yet in addition, there are three physical challenges—also tied to stress—that consistently and increasingly show up on my readers' radar. Allergies, attention deficit disorder (ADD), and childhood weight struggles all deserve special focus and attention in looking at causes and finding out methods for dealing with these issues that help both kids and Mom.

ALLERGIES 101

Grass, food, dust, pets—common allergy triggers hide innocently within our everyday. Why is it some of us suffer while others remain completely immune?

For severe allergy sufferers, like my son, Sam, these type of substances affect his every action and his total health and well-being. For Sam, this ordinarily harmless "stuff" becomes silent, secret, and perhaps even deadly invaders. When these "invaders" come into contact with my son, they are capable of triggering a dangerous explosion within his immune system, which can produce an outbreak of uncomfortable, potentially severe, symptoms. These blameless culprits, often innocently hidden from view, are much like a "minefield of triggers" for Sam to walk through every day.

As a nurse and a mother of an allergic child, I am acutely aware of the potential triggers that can elicit a reaction in him. My goal is to provide the best possible allergy-friendly environment for him, teach him how to be diligently alert to his allergic triggers, and in doing so, keep him in the best possible place of prevention to manage his sensitivity.

What is an allergy anyway?

The word *allergy* means "an altered reactivity." Unfortunately, it is now a common word in most people's vocabulary, though it wasn't back in the 1960s when the antibody known as IgE (one of many our bodies produce) was discovered to be the main culprit in classical allergic conditions.

Our body's intricate and complex defense system

An antibody is literally a personal bodyguard, a soldier cell produced naturally by the body to protect it from diseases or allergens. When these antibodies band together and attack, this is referred to as an "immune cell response." Now that the response is activated, the IgE antibody (fighter cell) attaches itself to a mast cell. A mast cell's job is actually to act like a bomb, causing an explosion. The newly produced IgE antibody becomes the "trip-wire" attached to the bomb, and when it is disturbed, it explodes.

> A mast cell's job is actually to act like a bomb, causing an explosion.

Histamine bomb

The explosion releases histamine into the bloodstream, which is what causes the sneezing, post-nasal drip, and itchy, watering eyes. In asthma, it is the histamine's effect on the smooth muscles of the bronchi (vital tubes that carry air to the lungs) that go into spasm, causing the classic "wheezing."

False alarm

Most of us have walked past a blaring car alarm; when we do we know most likely the triggered alarm was set off by an innocent event, such as a strong wind or an accidental bump. This same scenario is often true with an allergic response. The mast cell, acting as the alarm, is triggered by an innocent substance (such as pollen, grass, or dust) yet nevertheless trips the alarm to sound. The malfunctioning gene of an allergy-sensitive body thinks the harmless substance is an unwanted invader. Though it's misinformation, our body is trying only to protect us. Unfortunately, our system is activated and our body responds to the false alarm, releasing its histamine explosion along with its annoying repercussions that we experience as allergy symptoms.

Indoor air more polluted than outdoor

As a little girl growing up in a small Midwestern town, I can still hear my mother saying, "Open the windows, and let's bring some fresh air into the house." Now I am the mom, living in a large metropolis tagged as one of the most challenging places to live with allergies. Yet, as bad as that outside air might be, surprisingly, it's the indoor air that is much worse. According to the Environmental Protection Agency (EPA), our indoor air quality is four to five times worse than our polluted outdoor air. What's a mother to do?

WHY DO WE CARE?

Fast facts about asthma according to the Asthma and Allergy Foundation

- It is estimated 20 million Americans suffer from asthma.
- American children suffer from asthma more than any other chronic illness.
- Fifty percent of asthma cases are caused by airborne allergens.
- Asthma is the number-one cause of school absenteeism and costs our health care system $18 billion annually.

Weighing in

With twenty-five years of experience as a health care professional, an advocate for healthy living, and as a mother of an allergic child—my passion and approach lies in helping others help themselves in managing allergies. One of my favorite topics, of course, is how to maintain our bodies (and our children's) in a place of strength, allowing them to perform as nature intended, allowing them to self-heal from a place of prevention, medication-free.

Our body is like a reservoir

In understanding the way allergic triggers can affect us, I like to use the example of comparing our body to a reservoir. In regards to our environment, life presents us many different scenarios. Sometimes our environmental conditions are controllable (such as our home) and sometimes they are not (school or work). For an allergy sensitive person, our environment affects the "reservoir." Different factors can affect the reservoir: high pollen, grass or mold count, and pet dander, to name a few. Exposure to these factors fills the reservoir, and when the reservoir is full, it causes the dam to break. The allergy sufferer's body is able to handle one trigger perhaps, but the combination of too many factors—several triggers in the environment, stress, or a period of poor eating habits—tips it over the edge. When the dam breaks, the symptoms of an allergic response appear: running nose, itchy watery-eyes, eczema, wheezing, and asthma. This analogy may help explain why it's hard to predict your body's allergic reaction and why it can sometimes be more severe than others.

Allergy-proofing your home is doable

Creating the best possible environment in our home is one positive step we can take to help our families lower their "reservoir" and manage their allergies from a place of prevention. Decreasing the exposure of these pesky allergy-triggers can make a significant, sometimes almost magical, difference in your allergy "reservoir." The good news: Allergy-proofing your home is within everyone's reach and doable.

Where do I start?

There are numerous ideas when it comes to allergy-proofing your home. I focus on eliminating the top three allergic triggers: dust and dust mites, pet dander, and mold. The following three suggestions come from my research and personal experience in creating the best "allergy-trigger-free" environment for my family.

HERE ARE SOME OF MY FAVORITES

· **Allergy-free bedroom: Use allergy-free bedding, remove curtains/carpets, eliminate stuffed toys**

You will spend one-third of your life in bed. Therefore, it makes sense to create a sleeping environment that is as allergy-free as possible. Dust mites lurk in bedding, soft furnishings and high pile carpet. Invest in allergy-free bedding which encases your pillow and mattress. Wash your bedding and one chosen stuffed toy once a week in hot water (160 degrees F) or put the toy in a plastic bag in the freezer overnight. Remove carpets and curtains and replace with wood, tile or elements that don't hold dust and mites.

· **Damp dust weekly**

Use a damp micro fiber cloth to pick up any accumulated dust. A feather duster or dry cloth only pushes the dust around.

· **Pets live outside, or at a minimum, out of the bedroom**

Dander from your dog or cat can float around in the air and be a trigger for allergies. Thirty-six percent of Americans have dogs and 31 percent have cats. Cat allergens especially are "sticky" and adhere to clothing and other surfaces. If you're going to have pets, at a minimum, keep your pets out of the allergy sufferer's bedroom.

· **Clean duct work**

Having ducts cleaned by a reputable firm, and changing filters on your heating and AC units makes good sense. HEPA filters trap smaller particles and allergens.

· **A whole-house air filtration system**

This is an excellent avenue, which fits on your existing heating and cooling unit. The one-time cost is quickly absorbed as you no longer have to replace HEPA filters, and studies show it removes 99 percent of allergy triggers, such as dust, pet dander, mold, etc.

The bottom line

If the above suggestions appear drastic, just keep in mind the benefit ratio of incorporating some of these changes in exchange for living a potentially healthier, allergy-free life. Creating the best, allergy-trigger-free environment contributes to keeping your environmental "reservoir" low. Prevention is

The life of a child with ADD

We all know the drill—daily routine of school, activities, dinner, homework, and crawling into bed—sleepy, but hopefully happy. Maybe not quite the same for a child with classic ADD behavior problems: A sleepy, agitated kid who once again had trouble falling asleep the night before is now unable to focus on homework and beginning to feel anxious about another sleepless night. The child's anxiety is building as he feels the demands of yet another day of unmet expectations. What may be a typical day for some turns quickly into a repetitive nightmare for a child with ADD and his family.

Eight-year-old Michael was chronically unable to fall asleep at night. He and his mother came to me on the recommendation of her son's psychologist on the hope I could help him learn how to relax. And it wasn't just Michael who was suffering. His exhausted mother, Melanie, spent an additional two to four hours every night trying to get him to nod off.

Teaching relaxation

One Saturday morning Melanie and Michael arrived at my office ready to try yoga, breathing, and visualization techniques as a means of finding relief from the cycle of fatigue, irritation, and high emotions for both mother and child. I always feel teaching a mother and child together is a natural approach. In these exercises children have the instinctive ability to focus on their breath and watch how their body responds, they make it seem so effortless and simple—child's play, a great example for mothers to follow.

A life skill

Mothers and children who really want to make a change, and will commit to incorporating these techniques into their life, find relief. Dr. Carol Brady, a clinical psychologist in Houston, Texas, treats numerous children each month with ADD and has this to say about treatments that work: "In the practice of psychotherapy we are always looking for what works. I have found useful additional methods which complement traditional psychotherapy—yoga and breathing techniques being foremost among them." The reason these practices work, according to Brady, is that, "One of the classic behavioral problems with ADD is not paying attention to one's body signals and feelings, and it restricts a child's ability to have a balanced and honest view of their own body and reactions to others."

Comfortable in your own skin

Yoga, breathing, visualization, and relaxation are tools to bring about self-awareness—creating "comfort in your own skin." A small investment of time can reap big benefits in combating daily wear in an overstimulated, multi-tasking world. Who couldn't benefit in learning ways to "undo" your body at the end of the day preparing you for a much-needed restful sleep? As for Melanie and Michael, after a couple of weeks of dedicated practice, they both began getting some much-needed rest.

COMMON SENSE TIPS FOR GOOD LIVING—WHETHER YOU HAVE ATTENTION DEFICIT DISORDER OR NOT

Edward (Ned) Hallowell is an advocate and authority on ADD. Whether or not your child has ADD, his six lifestyle interventions in the management of ADD make good common sense for us all:

- **Positive human contact.** Due to our disconnected culture, people these days don't get enough smiles, hugs, waves hello, and warm handshakes. Positive human contact is as important as, if not more so than, a good night's sleep or a proper diet.

- **Reduce electronics** (e.g., television, video games, the Internet). Studies have shown that too much "electronic time" predisposes children to ADD.

- **Sleep.** Enough sleep is the amount of sleep that allows you to wake up without an alarm clock. Without enough sleep you'll act like you have ADD, whether or not you have it.

- **Diet.** Eat a balanced diet. Eat protein as part of breakfast. Protein is the best long-lasting source of brain fuel. Don't self-medicate with drugs, alcohol, or carbohydrates.

- **Exercise.** Regular exercise is one of the best tonics you can give your brain. Even if it's just walking for fifteen minutes, exercise every day. Exercise stimulates the production of epinephrine, dopamine, and serotonin, as do the medications we treat ADD with. Exercising is like taking medication for ADD in a holistic, natural way.

- **Prayer or meditation.** Both of these help to calm and focus the mind.

Did you know in America the width of an airline seat is 31-36 inches wide, while in China they are 29-28 inches? We don't need to know this statistic to know that America is overweight. According to the Surgeon General, nearly two out of every three Americans are overweight or obese. Unfortunately, that translates to one in three children being overweight in the USA.

CHILDHOOD OBESITY

Did you know in America the width of an airline seat is 31–36 inches, while in China they are 28–29 inches? We don't need to know this statistic to know that America is overweight. According to the Surgeon General, nearly two out of every three Americans are overweight or obese. Unfortunately, that translates to one in three children being overweight in the U.S. It is our fastest-growing cause of disease and death in America. Not only is being overweight physically devastating for children, but emotionally as well. The being "fat" label brings many self-esteem issues that compound the problem. And, it's completely preventable.

Kids are eating too much and exercising too little

One of the biggest concerns with the staggering statistic of childhood obesity is not only the immediate negative health repercussions, but also the groundwork being laid for further health issues like diabetes, high blood pressure, high cholesterol, and stressed joints. There may be some genetic or hormonal causes leading to childhood obesity, but the bottom line is this: Excess weight is caused by kids eating too much and exercising too little.

Simply, lifestyle has changed

It's no surprise why Americans have fallen off the rails when it comes to healthy living—simply put, it's a lifestyle change. Nowadays, hardly any children walk to school, eat an apple as a snack, or play outside until dark. Instead our food choices—super-sized fast food portions, processed foods with high amounts of sugar and hydrogenated fat—added to hours spent in front of an X-Box, all add up to excessive weight.

What does it mean to be overweight?

BMI (Body Mass Index) is an estimate of body fat using height and weight measurements. It is a way to determine how appropriate a child's weight is for a certain height and age. Even though you can calculate your BMI yourself, it is a good idea to chat with your doctor or nutritionist, who can interpret it over time as your child grows, instead of focusing on a number. A child with a large frame and lots of muscle will have a higher BMI, and alternatively a small frame may have a normal BMI but can still be carrying excess body fat.

Tip the scales in your favor

If the scales aren't tipping in your child's favor—try some of these ideas to get your child back on track:

- **Support your child.** As a mother, your role is crucial. Take every opportunity to gently encourage your child's self-esteem; building his confidence from the inside out is crucial in changing or modifying any habit or behavior. Point out what you see him do well. Talk to him about his feelings.

- **Respect your body.** Teach your child to honor her body. Basic principles of healthy living involve holding a reverence to eat well, exercise, and maintain confidence. They are all connected.

- **Improve the whole family exercise routine.** If everyone is exercising it helps motivate your child. That may be that extra push he needs to get up and get moving. Something as simple as an after supper walk around the block can be a great first step. Family bowling night, Sunday afternoon bike ride, or even walking around the zoo can be fun and an easy ways to get your blood pumping without even trying.

- **Focus on the positive.** Find ways to acknowledge your child's accomplishments that do not involve food: Instead of an ice cream treat, how about a trip to the park? Emphasize eating fresh and seasonal foods, take them to the farmers' market or grocery store and get them involved in making their own healthy choices.

- **Eating awareness.** Help them become aware of mindless eating, such as in front of the TV. Teach them to eat mindfully and eat with awareness, to not eat out of boredom or for comfort.

- **Keep a food diary.** According to a study in the *American Journal of Preventive Medicine* (Aug 2008), the more the participants wrote in their journals, the more weight they lost—about twice as much as those who didn't keep a journal. By keeping a simple food diary, you become more aware of how much you are eating and therefore more accountable for what you eat. It can also help identify hidden feelings that can lead to emotional overeating.

- **Set a good example.** Maybe one of the most important points in helping your child is cleaning up your own habits. It's hard to tell your kids to eat healthy and get some exercise if it isn't happening with you. When I first changed some of my more unhealthy eating habits for the better—everyone in my family benefited. Avoid food power struggles and lead by example, and everyone becomes a winner.

- **Be patient.** Do not worry if your child goes through some chubby phases. All three of my children seemed to have spurts of gaining some weight only to be followed by a spurt in height. Don't let any good intentions of focusing on your child's weight backfire, making you wish you'd never opened Pandora's box—possibly causing more harm than good.

YOU ARE WHAT YOU EAT

Regard your body as sacred, as if it were a temple. When making choices of "what to allow into your temple," choose wholesome, natural, complex carbohydrates combined with protein. An apple with cheese, a handful of nuts with a glass of milk, or whole grain toast with high quality peanut butter are quick and easy fast food. These types of complex carbohydrates combined with protein give you a fighting chance, enabling you with a steady flow of energy throughout your day.

Chapter 5: The Big Three: Difficult Challenges for Today's Kids

Q: *My allergies seems so unpredictable. Why do my symptoms seem to get better and worse? I never used to have any problems with allergies, and now I do? Why is that?*

A: In understanding the way allergic triggers can affect us, I like to compare the body to a reservoir. In regards to our environment, life presents us many different scenarios. Sometimes our environmental conditions are controllable (such as our home) and sometimes they are not (school or work). For an allergy sensitive person, our environment affects the "reservoir." Different factors can affect the reservoir: high pollen, grass or mold count, and pet dander to name a few. Exposure to these factors fills the reservoir, and when the reservoir is full, it causes the dam to break. The allergy sufferer's body is able to handle one trigger perhaps, but the combination of too many factors—several triggers in the environment, stress, or a period of poor eating habits—tips it over the edge. When the dam breaks, the symptoms of an allergic response appear: running nose, itchy watery-eyes, eczema, wheezing, and asthma. This analogy may help explain why it's hard to predict your body's allergic reaction and why it can sometimes be more severe than others.

Q: *How can yoga, breathing or relaxation techniques help my son's ADD?*

A: To reference Dr. Carol Brady, the behavioral expert we met in this chapter, tells us that "One of the classic behavioral problems with ADD is not paying attention to one's body signals and feelings, and it restricts a child's ability to have a balanced and honest view of their own body and reactions to others." With this in mind, yoga, breathing, visualization, and relaxation are tools to bring about self-awareness—creating "comfort in your own skin." A small investment of time can reap big benefits in combating daily wear in an over-stimulated, multi-tasking world.

Q: *My twelve-year-old daughter is probably 30 pounds overweight. What should I do?*

A: In my opinion, one of the best and easiest interventions you can do as her mother is lead by example. It's hard to tell your kids to eat healthy and get some exercise if this lifestyle isn't happening with you. When I first changed some of my more unhealthy eating habits for the better, everyone in my family benefited. Avoid food power struggles, praise her healthy actions and lead by example and everyone becomes a winner.

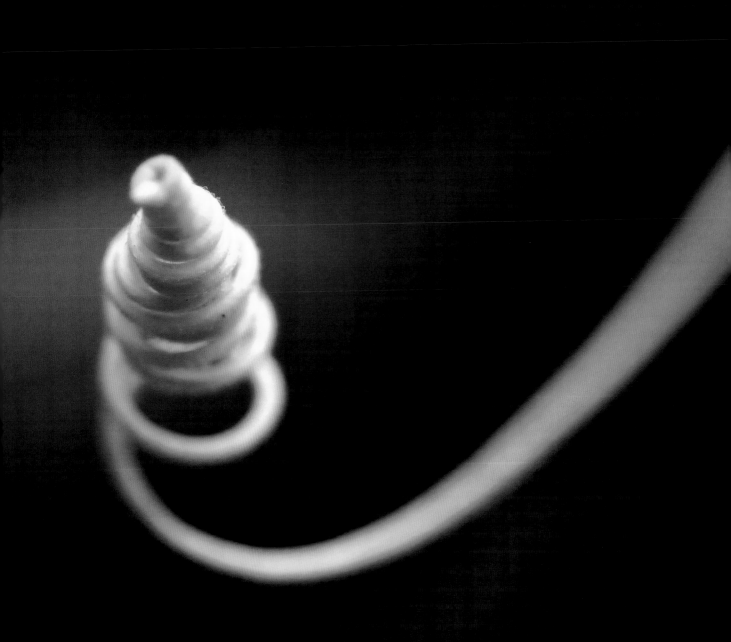

6

Going Green

Recently, one of the world's finest violinists played at a Washington DC metro station. For nearly an hour during rush hour he played Bach, gloriously. Thousands of people passed by as he played, and hardly a soul paid any attention, save a few children who were pushed to move on. Two days prior, this same man, Joshua Bell, one of the world's most famous violinists, sold out a packed theater of $100 seats. This is a true story, the experiment organized by the *Washington Post* to explore people's perceptions and priorities.

Reading about this story made me stop and think about how I perceive beauty in a commonplace environment. Would I have been one of those "passersby?" Maybe. Do I appreciate and recognize beautiful sensations around me? What does this experiment teach me? If I were unable to stop and listen to one of the best musicians in the world playing some of the finest music ever written, how many other sights and sounds have I missed along the way?

NATURE'S ORCHESTRA

For me, nature and my relationship and responsibility to it feels much the same; I want to be responsive to its beauty, whether it's leading my kids through example in my efforts of recycling, eating organic food, or using vinegar instead of a chemical-based cleaner. In nature, the grass continues to grow, leaves fall, snowflakes flurry, and the sun shines all in its own time, whether I notice this beauty—or not. Paying attention to the ecosystem and it's intricate synchronicity is like the listening to the finest orchestra being played all on its own—it's up to me to notice and care.

We are connected

We are connected to our world—the water I drink, the air I breathe, the food I eat, or the sun that shines on my face. It is part of me and I am part of it. And, like those who hurried past the unnoticed musician, I am the loser for not paying attention. The difference is that if I continue to be part of the crowd passing by, not taking any notice, then eventually one day the music may stop. I am as much a part of the ecosystem as any one piece of the band. And, as a mother leading my family to health and wellbeing, how can I not hear the music and take responsibility to preserve something so intricately linked and sacred?

> To appreciate beauty; to find the best in others; to leave the world a bit better whether
>
> by a healthy child, a garden patch, or a redeemed social condition;
>
> to know even one life has breathed easier because you lived.
>
> This is to have succeeded. — **Ralph Waldo Emerson**

Are you wondering how you can teach your children compassion, responsibility, and their connection to the plant that sustains them? It may be easier than you think. If your current "green" habits are strong, perhaps some of the following ideas will inspire; if going green is something that means starting from scratch, take a simple first step within your everyday habits—little steps build, and your children will happily follow in your tracks.

RECYCLE: MAKE IT AN EVERYDAY HABIT

A few years ago on a summer trip to Canada, I was literally stopped in my tracks with the realization of how my family isn't up to par with our efforts in contributing to such an essential way of living. I opened my friend's kitchen cupboard to look for the trashcan. In my amazement I found something that hardly resembled the double-wide I have at my home. Their trashcan was the size of a child's small plastic pail, the kind a child might use when collecting shells at the beach. I was surprised at first, and then came a rush of guilt. The pail under their sink was so small, so cute. The trash can(s) at my home were four times this size. Our Canadian friends recycle. I thought we did too! The difference is they recycle absolutely everything—plastic, paper, glass, and they have a compost pile. That tiny bucket in their cupboard held their un-recyclable items. They made their everyday recycling habit appear so effortless. A family of five fit its week's trash into this adorable little pail.

Fell off the wagon

Moving to Houston, Texas has brought many opportunities and friendships—however, it initially wasn't very good for my family's recycling habits. Our neighborhood didn't promote recycling and we initially fell off the wagon and only recycled paper. It was so easy not to—we somehow just slipped out of the habit. Even I, who come from a strong lineage of recyclers. My dad had us crushing aluminum cans and rolling newspapers logs for the fireplace ever since I was a little girl. And, during the fifteen years we lived in England we joined in with a dedicated nation of fierce recyclers—as it was very convenient, easy, and everyone did it.

Why should we bother?

That summer trip shook me into the realization of my period of denial. I needed to get back on the path of recycling and teach my children (as I had been taught) through example—creating another generation of recyclers. Recycling has so many benefits, but two of the biggest are that it saves energy and prevents hazardous materials from ending up in the landfill.

In regards to energy, to create everyday products, such as papers, cans and plastics, a lot of fossil fuel is used, and therefore emissions, which of course in turn creates pollution. Recycling allows a more efficient use of resources. The more products we can recycle, the more energy we save for the planet and society as a whole. Period.

Recycling also prevents hazardous materials and chemicals, such as lead and mercury, from ending up in landfills, and potentially into our water supply. There are hazardous risks associated with our trash—including those you may not initially think of recycling. Things like batteries, electronics, motor oil, paint and any product that has "Caution" or "Warning" on the label need to be recycled. We can agree that recycling is good for the Earth, but it is also good for the family.

A family affair: Start small and build—it's contagious

When we moved into our neighborhood we faithfully kept our paper products in bags by the back door and dropped them at the children's school. Gradually, we moved back into the groove of being full-fledged recyclers where the whole family contributes. Our daughters, Allie and Sarah, volunteered to take turns delivering the recycling each week to our nearby recycling center, something that even to this day they do without complaint. Sam is in charge of crushing aluminum cans and breaking down boxes, while my husband Ron and I rinse and sort. We have a nice little recycling station made simply out of a few bins in our garage where we sort our plastic, glass, and paper. It's a family project that I honestly never imagined would work so seamlessly. Everyone participates and the kid's contagious response to our efforts was something I hadn't anticipated. Kids seem to learn from actions rather than words—I feel once they "get it"—why it's important to protect and nourish their planet, they get into the flow and often remind me saying, "Don't forget to recycle that, Mom!" making the process easier than you may think. A good friend of mine has a two-year-old at a Montessori preschool who can direct you about what goes in the compost bin and what goes in the recycling bin!

Here are some facts and my favorite tips to kick-start you into the "recycling club":

- **Paper products make up 40 percent of all trash.** Translation: Paper is probably the easiest product to recycle. So if everyone managed to just recycle paper products, almost half of our trash would then be recycled! Simply commit to place a bag by your back door to put your junk mail and daily papers in—that is a huge step. Or eliminate the problem altogether (see Four Million Tons of Junk Mail).

- **Americans throw away twenty-five trillion Styrofoam cups** that cannot be decomposed or be recycled. Think about the next time you use Styro—is there an alternative you could have chosen?

- **Americans throw away 2.5 million plastic bottles every hour!** That is a lot of plastic. Treat yourself and your child to a metal water bottle—there are so many really cool ones available. Stop buying plastic water bottles. It will save you time, money, and the environment.
- **Cell phones, computers, and other technology release toxins** into the environment when they are thrown away. The only way to stop that pollution is to recycle them. Check out your local electronic recycling center—and head that way next time you have something to get rid of.

TIPS TO GET YOU STARTED

My family and I may have fallen off the recycling wagon for a short while—but we came back in full force and with a renewed passion for recycling with a fresh approach. You can too.

- **Make the decision to start recycling** and ask your family if they are interested in joining in with you on the effort. Chances are, your kids will be more enthusiastic than you!
- **Start with small steps.** Put a paper bag somewhere convenient and use it exclusively as a paper-product trash can. Your child's school should have some sort of recycling drop-off station and is an effortless place to toss your paper on the way to or from school.
- **Recycle your printer cartridges.** Take them to your local computer store for a discount on a new cartridge or paper. Do not put them in the trashcan.
- **Consider starting up some recycling in your school.** See Resources for ideas on how to begin. Kids catch on quickly and soon become some of your best advocates.
- **If you are not recycling already,** find out if you live in a curbside recycling area. If so, request a bin and they will pick up your recycle curbside!

See Resources for more great tips on how to go green.

RECYCLING SYMBOL

Recycling is the process of taking a product at the end of its useful life and using all or part of it to make another product. This is the recognized symbol for recycling. Each arrow represents a different part of the recycling process, from collection to re-manufacture to resale.

FOUR MILLION TONS OF JUNK MAIL

Every day when I reach into my mailbox, usually about half of what I pull out is junk mail. In the U.S. four million tons of junk mail goes out every year. Recycling is one way to help, but what about nipping it in the bud and go directly to the source?

According to Consumer Research Institute—if you take a few minutes to stop unwanted mail, it will give you back as many as 70 hours per year spent sorting and trashing or recycling your unwanted mail! What mom couldn't use some extra time in her day, with the added bonus of helping the environment? Plus eliminating extra junk mail can only lead to a more peaceful space as I talk about later in creating a peaceful home. **Check out Resources (page 168) to help you eliminate the junk.**

HEALTHY FOOD CHOICES

What is organic anyway?

 I am frequently asked about what to eat as part of a healthy lifestyle plan—clients, readers, members of an audience ask, "With so many choices, its overwhelming to know what to do?" Even though I dedicate an entire chapter to providing what I feel are some of the most important points in good nutrition—I still think many people have the question, what does it mean to eat organic, and is that the same thing as eating whole foods?

What organic means

I understand a healthy mother just wants to know: What is organic? Why should I bother? Most importantly, in a time where tightening the purse strings is not only a good idea, but likely necessary: Is buying organic worth my health, my money?

Understanding a few definitions can help you make the right organic choices for your family. Here are some important facts to know. According to the USDA, organic farming requires the producer to grow and transport the goods without using synthetic chemicals or pesticides, and to avoid genetically modification and synthetic fertilizers. Raising organic meat requires the farmer to avoid antibiotics, growth hormones, or feed made from animal byproducts. The animals are required to have access to the outdoors.

UNDERSTAND WHAT THE LABEL MEANS

- **On packaged foods, "100% Organic"** means that the product must contain 100 percent organic ingredients.

- **"Organic" means** that at least 95 percent of ingredients are organically produced.

- **"Made with Organic Ingredients"** requires that at least 70 percent of ingredients are organic. The remaining ingredients must come from an approved list created by the USDA.

- **"Free-range" or "Free-roaming"** is a misleading term seen on meat, poultry and eggs. This simply means that outdoor access was available for some time each day; it is likely that the animal did not spend much time outdoors, if any.

- **"All-natural"** is probably the most misleading marketing tag of all! For meat and poultry, USDA defines "natural" as not containing any artificial flavoring, colors, chemical preservatives, or synthetic ingredients. If it is any other product, it is completely up to the manufacturer whether they want to package it with this label.

Start slow, begin to read a few labels while shopping and learn to recognize these key words. Soon you will develop a keen eye for noticing the authentic organic seal of approval.

Which fruits and vegetables should I buy organic?

Researchers at the Environmental Working Group found that even after washing, the "dirty dozen" consistently carry much higher levels of pesticides than other fruits and vegetables.

Organic foods generally cost more than their mass-produced counterparts; after all, they are grown in smaller crops, and additionally have lower yields because organic farmers aren't using chemicals. However, organic buying can boil down to knowing where it's important to pay the extra. Unlike the "dirty dozen," these fruits and veggies generally do not have pesticide residue after a good washing.

CLEAN AND GREEN	THE DIRTY DOZEN
Pesticides Diminished After Washing	*The USDA's Must-Buy Organics*
Fruit	*Fruit*
Bananas	Apples
Kiwi	Cherries
Mangos	Grapes, imported (Chile)
Papaya	Nectarines
Pineapples	Peaches
	Pears
Vegetables	Raspberries
Asparagus	Strawberries
Avocado	
Broccoli	*Vegetables*
Cauliflower	Bell peppers
Corn	Celery
Onions	Potatoes
Peas	Spinach

PLASTIC BOTTLES? THINK AGAIN.

Plastics are made from petroleum and other non-biodegradable materials, meaning that unless they are recycled, they will remain plastic bottles for at least the next thousand years. When thrown in a garbage can, they make their way to a landfill with the rest of the trash. With Americans estimated to have thrown out 4.62 pounds of trash per day in 2007, the amount of plastics that will be sitting in landfills is truly mind-boggling. Not to mention that research links the chemical BPA found in some plastic bottles hazardous to your health.

Other organic products I feel are worth considering as part of incorporating a healthy lifestyle for your families include milk products, beef, poultry, and eggs. Studies by the World Health Organization link the use of antibiotics in animal products with increased bacterial resistance in humans, in addition to the issue of artificial growth hormones. Children, pregnant women and the unborn are thought to be most susceptible to the negative health effects of beef and dairy cattle injected with artificial hormones. Hormone residues in beef have played havoc in the early onset of puberty in girls. Buying organically raised products is a good way to avoid these unwanted hormones and byproducts. In my own family, we put extra money into the highest quality food we can afford; I feel we are worth it!

The average dairy cow produced almost 5,300 pounds of milk a year in 1950, today, a typical cow produces more than 18,000 pounds.

The 411 on Pesticides

Children's immune systems, which are less developed than adults, are at greater risk from high levels of pesticide use. Studies conducted in 2003 by the Centers for Disease Control and Prevention detected twice the level of pesticides in children as compared to adults. Mothers of young children and pregnant women are especially vulnerable and should really make the effort to buy organic, as numerous scientific studies link chemicals to cancer, autism, ADD, allergies, and asthma.

What about baby?

Bisphenol-A, commonly known as BPA, is an ingredient found in some plastic sippy cups, baby bottles, and water bottles. The *Journal of the American Medical Association* indicated that elevated levels of BPA could cause heart disease, liver failure and diabetes. More worrying, the National Toxicology Program cautions that BPA may cause babies to develop abnormally. The research is such that Andrew Weil, a physician and pioneer in integrative medicine who has been on the leading edge of BPA concerns for decades, works to recommend and develop products that minimize these health risks. In 2008, the National Resources Defense Council (NRDC) found that the current level of evidence is sufficient to issue a public health warning to reduce BPA exposure for prevention of adverse effects. Many authorities along with Dr Weil have been speaking about the issues of using products that contain BPA. Canada has banned the use of BPA in baby products. The good news is—it's simple to prevent. When purchasing plastics, avoid plastics labeled "#7," which are most likely to contain the chemical and buy products labeled "BPA FREE".

What about your baby's food?

When Sam was a baby, due to his allergies, I made his baby food. I can still remember mashing batches of sweet potatoes, peas, and carrots, and freezing them in ice cube trays for later to use as needed. I remember the whole process; it didn't feel that difficult, just part of the routine. If you have an allergy-sensitive child, it's best to hold off on solid foods until they are six months old when their immune systems are more mature. Every mother wants the very best for her baby—that first bite of anything to be pure and perfect. In my opinion, baby food that is free of pesticides and other added chemicals is optimal. There are numerous studies that pesticides do, in fact, more adversely affect children and pregnant women. Dr. Alan Greene, MD, one of America's most loved pediatricians noted for "giving real answers to parents questions" and author of numerous books, including *Raising Baby Green*, says, " We have a window of opportunity to introduce flavors to infants they will enjoy for a lifetime." He goes on to explain that up until thirteen months a baby's taste buds welcome new tastes, but after this time it's an innate response for the toddler to reject any new taste offered. This dislike is actually a built-in defense mechanism to protect the toddler from all the things he wants to put into his mouth at this stage, which naturally protects him from poisons. As mothers, I feel it is important to seize this golden window of opportunity and feed your baby the best possible food.

Easy tips to get you started

- **Cooked, fresh vegetables and stewed fruits** are best (besides bananas or other soft fruits that can be mashed). Steaming is probably the best method—it loses the least nutrients/vitamins.
- **Do not sweeten** or season your baby's food.
- **Freeze what you don't use** in an ice cube tray. It gives you individual, easily accessible portions for later.
- **If making your own seems like too much work**—a week's worth of baby food can be made in about thirty minutes. Plus add in the advantage of saving money.
- **According to the American Academy of Pediatrics,** beets, turnips, carrots, collard greens, and spinach all potentially contain large amount of nitrates from pesticides; these chemicals can cause anemia in young infants. Buy organic vegetables and make your own.

NOT SO GUILTY

If you are a healthy mother with a bit of a sweet tooth—raw chocolate has been shown to be extraordinarily high in Vitamin C, and an excellent source of magnesium, chromium and iron. Best of all, organic raw cacao is full of disease-preventing antioxidants—containing even more than green tea or red wine. Although don't stock up on just any chocolate bar—the milk contained in most chocolates actually decreases all these amazing benefits; so reach for the dark chocolate. Look for packages that mention 60 percent or more cacao to maximize those delicious benefits.

EATING FRESH AND HEALTHY

Getting kids to eat fruits and vegetables, whether they are organic or not, can be challenging. These methods are not only great ways to get your kids to eat their peas, they are fun ways to educate your kids about where food comes from, demonstrate the ideas of growing and eating food locally, and seasonal eating.

Container gardening: herbs and cutting flowers

My kids and I have always enjoyed puttering around in the garden. We religiously planted our sunflower seeds that within a few months sprouted to be taller than them, potted herbs, and a flower-cutting garden. We even grew lettuce in a pot—try it, it's easy and then fun to eat. When my kids were little it was an exciting way to get them involved in the process of watching a flower or vegetable develop from a seed into a mature plant, with the added experience of having helped "bring to life and harvest" what they were going to eat. Nothing was more sacred than that bite of lettuce, sprig of rosemary, or flower they had nurtured and watch multiply—now cut and brought into the house to enjoy. It not only provided them with a sense of accomplishment, from watering and "praying" for its growth—it allowed them to take part in and understand the sacredness of life and respect the food they ate. See Resources for lots of how-tos.

Go local at a farmer's market

Another way to bring fresh healthy food into your family's life is an outdoor market. Farmer's markets are a wonderful way to support your local community and help the environment by reducing the amount of food trucked across the country. It is a great place to buy beautiful produce, as well as provide a fantastic outing for you and your family. Our kids have always enjoyed Saturday markets. I remember Sarah as a little girl talking to a tall, gentle farmer about the eggs he had for sale. She respectfully listened to his story of collecting the eggs and which hens where his best "producers." Fresh markets almost always have live music, nice food available to eat, and an atmosphere that connects us to the season. It makes for an effortless way to stay in touch with good fresh food, leading your children right along with you. See Resource section for an effortless way to find local markets and restaurants that serve locally sourced ingredients.

Picking farm

Every October my teenagers still enjoy choosing and carving their own pumpkins and roasting the seeds. In years past, when the kids were little we spent many summer afternoons in the fields of picking farms—strawberries, blackberries, and apples were their favorites. Never have my children enjoyed their fruit or vegetable more than the pieces they have grown or picked themselves. Take a few hours and connect with nature, get some exercise, and get out and have some fun.

CREEPY CRAWLERS

Composting is an earth-friendly way of getting rid of your kitchen waste and turning it into beneficial, rich soil that goes on to nurture a new crop of food (or flowers). Composting with worms is an even more fun project for kids—especially little boys who delight in the "ick" factor. Worm composting consists of keeping worms in a bin with biodegradable material, while you "feed" the worms what would ordinarily go in the compost bin—scraps, peelings, and more. The worms digest the material, and after a few months, your compost and the worms' castings create vermicompost—one of the richest soil improvements Mother Nature provides. This is what you'll need to get started:

- a bin
- a supply of biodegradable bedding
- a supply of food waste
- worms!

Organic cleaning

Living in England, everyone was more environmentally conscious, and so natural cleaning was a topic most mothers were familiar with. It wasn't unusual to see moms using vinegar or lemons to clean their homes. Turns out, a load of chemicals are rather deceptively marketed as making our homes healthier places. Indeed, household cleaning products do keep our homes germ-free and squeaky-clean. However, many of these same products contain harsh chemicals that aren't good for our environment or for us, especially if anyone in your family suffers with allergies or sensitivities to chemicals.

Simply beautiful

Though making your own home cleansers may sound daunting, the recipes are easy and surprisingly versatile. Baking soda sprinkled in a toilet bowl and drizzled with vinegar makes a fantastic toilet bowl cleaner, and equal parts white vinegar and water can become your all-purpose cleaner; add in a lemon and you've got everything you need. With a few small changes, it is quite easy to phase out a majority of the harsh chemical cleaners under your sink. Save your money and the environment with the added bonus of eliminating the risk of poison for small children. If a kid swallows vinegar, he'll just make a sour face!

How to clean naturally—get back to basics

Get started by getting back to basics. Start with these five:

- **Microfiber cloth.** This fantastic little cloth gets the great all-around award for cleaning any surface and it just needs to be dampened with water. When it's dirty toss it into your washing machine.

- **Vinegar.** Equal parts vinegar and water become your spray bottle of disinfectant. Add a few drops of your essential oil (lavender, lemongrass or rosemary are great choices) and you have a disinfectant that smells good, too.

- **Baking soda.** Becomes your paste cleaner when sprinkled on a half of lemon. Smells fantastic and cleans even lime scale.

- **Lemon.** Use it with olive oil for furniture polish, or take a wedge and whiz around your sink to keep it squeaky clean.

- **Essential oil.** I use essential oils for many purposes besides cleaning, however they work well as cleaners and leave that lovely clean smell behind.

GOING GREEN

ESSENTIAL OILS

Pine: Pine oil is distilled from the needles of the evergreen tree. Because evergreens are naturally abundant, pine oil is relatively inexpensive. Pine is a clean, fresh scent, already popular in commercial cleaning products. Pine oil also contains phenols, which have germ-killing properties. Mix with vinegar and water for your all-purpose cleaner.

Eucalyptus: Eucalyptus is another disinfectant with a powerful scent. I love the smell and use it throughout the house.

Orange: Orange oil is a natural cleanser as well, and it smells zesty and refreshing. Orange oil works great mixed as a floor cleaner, or mixed with baking soda as a carpet deodorizer.

Lemon: Lemon oil is another powerful cleaner; it is great mixed with olive oil for furniture polish.

Lemongrass: Lemongrass has a light citrus aroma and according to *The Essential Oils Desk Reference* also has antifungal and antibacterial properties.

Lavender: Gentle, soothing lavender is another popular scent. Lavender oil mixed with water makes a great linen refresher.

Chapter 6: Going Green

Q: *I share your passion for our ecosystem, however sometimes I feel that my small contribution doesn't really make a difference in the big picture. How can I feel more connected?*

A: As I mention at the beginning of this chapter, like those who hurried past the unnoticed musician, I am the loser for not paying attention. The difference is that if I continue to be part of the crowd passing by, not taking any notice, then eventually one day the music may stop. I am as much a part of the ecosystem as any one piece of the band. And, as a mother leading my family to health and wellbeing, how can I not hear the music and take responsibility to preserve something so intricately linked and sacred? That is true whether my efforts are toward recycling, eating organic food, or using vinegar instead of a chemical-based cleaner.

Q: *Organic fruits and veggies are more expensive. If I want to invest the extra money on organic produce, which fruits and vegetables should I buy organic?*

A: Researchers at the Environmental Working Group found that even after washing, the "dirty dozen" consistently carry much higher levels of pesticides than other fruits and vegetables. Organic buying can boil down to knowing where it's important to pay the extra money if you need to make a choice. Refer to the list on page 113 of this chapter.

Q: *I am a new mother and I want to buy baby bottles to use after I finish nursing. I have heard a lot lately about being careful with plastics carrying chemicals. Can you tell me more about that?*

A: Yes, Bisphenol-A, commonly known as BPA, is an ingredient found in some plastic sippy cups, baby bottles, and water bottles. The *Journal of the American Medical Association* indicated that elevated levels of BPA could cause heart disease, liver failure and diabetes. More worrying, the National Toxicology Program cautions that BPA may cause babies to develop abnormally. The good news is—it's simple to prevent. When purchasing plastics, avoid those labeled "#7," which are most likely to contain the chemical and buy products labeled "BPA FREE."

Q: *I really want to start using less chemicals in my home and especially with my cleaning products. It all feels too complicated. Can you make a few suggestions to get me started?*

A: I talk about how to clean naturally in this chapter and though making your own home cleansers may sound daunting, the recipes are easy and surprisingly versatile. Baking soda sprinkled in a toilet bowl and drizzled with vinegar makes a fantastic toilet bowl cleaner, and equal parts white vinegar and water can become your all-purpose cleaner; add in a lemon and you've got everything you need. With a few small changes, it is quite easy to phase out a majority of the harsh chemical cleaners under your sink. Save your money and the environment with the added bonus of eliminating the risk of poison for small children. If a kid swallows vinegar, he'll just make a sour face!

7

What Feeds Your Spirit?

A couple of years ago our twin daughters turned sixteen. Of course, I remember many wonderful moments from their birthday festivities; however, one I will never forget is the day they each slid a brand new driver's license into their purses. The girls got their first used-but-sturdy set of wheels, along with responsibility, freedom, and choices. Wow. *Yikes!*

Excitedly they drove off to school the next morning—without me! Still their mother, after all, I asked them to check in with me when they arrived at school. I prayed the entire twenty-minute journey and with a sigh of relief finally received their text: "Got 2 School. LUV U." The routine followed for the next week or so. Then one morning they forgot to text me, and I forgot to ask. It was OK, no news was good news, but I'm still surprised this big step happened so fast.

Take a back seat

A few weeks later we were getting ready to run some Saturday errands. Sarah announces, "Hey mom, I'll drive" and Sam chimes in "Yeah, I'll sit in the front with Sarah." Within a minute I was banished to the back seat, the seat normally reserved for our dog. Oh well, I thought, this will be a great opportunity to see how Sarah's driving has improved. As we screeched out of the driveway I grabbed the seat below me. Saying a prayer under my breath I tried to focus on my breathing, slow and deep. The music immediately cranked up to a level I never knew speakers could put out. I couldn't really hear anything except for the bass vibrating, and I began to feel invisible, nervous, afraid to speak. I was entering into an altered state, frozen in my feelings of fear and awe. And then something happened; I started to giggle. I guess it was some kind of a natural response to my stressed-out body that moved in to help me cope. The giggling freed me; it allowed me to surrender and let go. Sam and Sarah up in the front seat, oblivious to me in the back, chatting away, enjoying the lyrics of the song they had blasting, and traveling (very swiftly) down the road. I remained quiet with my little giggles for the duration of the journey. Sarah peeled into a very tight parking spot, stopped the car with a jolt, and looked back over her shoulder at me. With her soft brown eyes open wide she asked, "Hey mom, you were so quiet—what did you think of my driving?"

Unbuckling my seat belt, and slowly stepping onto the firm solid ground, I squeaked out, "Thanks for the ride."

One of my favorite films, *Finding Nemo,* features a turtle named Crush who talks about how to know when to let go of your kids. "You never really know, but when they know, you'll know, you know? And when you relax and go with the flow—Koo-Koo KaChoo they find their way back to the big old blue" he says with a surfer-dude drawl as they coast along with the Australian current, relaxing and going with the flow.

Ah, the wisdom of an animated character! Surrendering, letting go of the idea that I think I need to be, or can be, in control of my life's circumstances or my children's next chapter allows me room to live with the grace of each day. Sometimes it is my turn to drive, and sometimes it's my turn to take a back seat. Feeding my spirit begins from a place of having the wisdom to know the difference.

Everything happens for a reason

As I mention in Chapter 1, Sam's illness as a baby really rocked my world and brought with it a questioning of faith: why, I wondered, should an innocent little boy suffer so much? Sometimes, holding onto faith makes us feel blindly led, powerless, regardless of whether that faith is spiritual, religious, or simply personal. I like to think of faith as an intuitive knowing that everything happens for a reason and everything happens at the right time. Sometimes our hardest lessons are those that teach us how to grow the most. When life becomes stagnant or flat, there is no growth. Learning to accept this has softened me. It has allowed life to flow through me, and allowed me to embrace each day and experience for what it is—and to look for opportunities to grow. Sam was born in October, making his zodiac sign that of Libra. The symbol for Libra is a scale representing "balance." This little boy came into the world bringing with him many challenges and many gifts: One of those was to teach me the gift of balance.

I feel spirit as the light in my soul, a divine spark of inner peace and strength, enabling me to carry on through difficult times. As I reconnect with this flame deep inside me it warms through me from the inside with feelings of security, self-confidence, and steadfastness.

Just as I manually adjust the lens of my camera, universal truths such as, "In giving, we receive," "Do unto others, as you would do unto yourself," or "Seeing the divine beauty in all people and things," begin to feel organic and familiar, and come into focus when I reconnect to that inner part of me. There, right in front of me is a simple and beautiful image—one that was always there, but now brought into crisper focus. In this place, simple yet profound truths become easier to see and are effortlessly passed on to my children.

WHAT FEEDS YOUR SPIRIT?

What feeds your spirit? Sit back, relax and take a 360-degree view. If whatever you are currently doing to feed your soul works for you then keep doing it; use your routines, traditions, perhaps rituals of religion to feed you. Look to the common threads among belief systems instead of what separates them. There is a common vein, an underlying current that connects, surges through all traditions, uniting all of them with the common goal—opening your heart and mind to your own divine essence. Elizabeth Lesser, co-founder of Omega Institute, calls spirituality "an instinct," not something learned but something "already there inside us." That said, here are some proven methods for connecting with your spirit—unlocking your creative soul, doing vision work, playing like a child, spending time on your own, and finding quiet space in your mind through meditation or prayer —all of these clear out "clutter" of day-to-day living. These things work for me and can work for you and your children, helping you find a place of greater clarity and peace. I encourage you to incorporate time in everyday to connect with spirit, and by teaching your child to honor and respect this connection to spirit it gives them a rock to anchor upon.

Creative expression of the self

Creative self-expression is a powerful tool. It can provide an avenue that allows us to get in touch with the inner dialogue, the endless chatter in our head, having to almost stop and interrupt yourself, "Uh, excuse me, I can't seem to get a thought in edgewise." Butting into the mindless treadmill of constant thought we are able to *hear,* to get to the heart and soul of the matter, to feed our spirit. Following are a few of my favorite tools for unlocking some quiet space; even if it's just a brief opening, inspiration, clarity or matters of the heart can slip in. Following are some ideas to get you started. The good news—it's contagious! Once your children see you enjoying yourself all they want to do is join the fun.

Lose track of time

When I spend time doing something I really enjoy, I tend to lose track of time on the clock and enter into a detached space from my day-to-day life. In this free place, I can be at my best, and return to feeling happy for no real reason. It's child-like fun, simple and spontaneous, and it brings a powerful punch to addressing my stress and unlocking whatever may be trapped inside my subconscious mind.

The art as a process, not a product

As a little girl I played the piano. Off and on for most of my adult life I have entertained the idea of getting back into playing. Then, last year, I finally made the decision to rent a piano. I don't have a dedicated practice time. Every now and then I sit down and play a little. According to my family, I'm not that good, and they're right, but they do recognize that Mom loves to play! It is a welcomed release that allows me to tap into a part of me that could easily be forgotten. The sound of my music making isn't as valuable to me as the relaxed feeling it brings when I play. And, even though I cannot play some of the same soul-stirring songs I love to listen to—whether I am playing or listening, classical piano music contributes to a relaxing part of my day.

Tapping into natural healing

Time spent in a stress-free place allows your body to instinctively respond. Just like a teeter-totter, it finds it's way back to balance; a natural worry-free place brings equilibrium and steadiness back into play. It allows your body to play catch up—besides unlocking inspiration and creativity it also allows you to self-heal. "Many women feel guilty taking time for themselves, but for happiness and good health, you need an inspiring purpose," says Dr. Andrea Pennington, an integrative medicine physician and wellness coach. "A good hobby makes you lose all sense of time and self, liberating you from the everyday." Taking time out to lose yourself in a favorite pastime is like stepping out of a loud, crowded, smoke-filled room and taking a long, deep inhalation of fresh air.

HEALING HOBBIES

The ideas below are just a few meant to inspire you. Let them guide you to create some fun that naturally heals you, passing on the benefits to your children and letting you enjoy being a kid all over again.

- **Think like a kid.** What activities did you do as a child—play an instrument, paint, or dance?

- **Create a vision board.** According to my friend Lucia Capacchione, author of *The Art of Emotional Healing* and corporate consultant to Walt Disney, "You can create the life you want by focusing on the feelings you want and then picturing the realization of your dreams through the use of magazine-photo collages." My children and I have created vision boards for years. We all keep them and love to look back and see how many things come true—it's amazing!

- **Include the family.** Lose yourself in a good, old-fashioned card or board game, or work a jigsaw puzzle. Or, take it outside and shoot some hoops with your child, or enjoy a family walk, hike, or bike ride.

- **Get out in nature.** How about filling up some bird feeders, get a book on local birds, or take in the naturally healing effects of digging in the dirt with potting or gardening?

VISION BOARDS

Material: Art paper, scissors, glue and collage material

How to:

1. **Choose a theme.** What do feel is lacking in your life? What would you like to create more of? Try to use one word and title your board. You can always make more than one.

2. **Dedicate some time.** Spend an hour or so on a Saturday afternoon at the kitchen table or outside on a picnic table, and invite your kids to join you.

3. **Enjoy the process.** You can't do it wrong. Look through magazines, use mottos or photographs, even arts and craft supplies to create a board for your vision.

4. **When finished, display your board** in a place where you can see it regularly. Encourage your children to do the same. Kids are typically very proud of their work. When you look at it, think about your word and how that feels—how the images represent this to you in your life.

WHY JOURNAL?

Journaling is a great way to hear what is going on inside your head; sometimes we don't even know what is on our mind until we write our thoughts down. As Anne Frank reminds us, "Paper is more patient than man."

When Allie and Sarah were in junior high I asked them to help me write about journaling. I knew both of them did it and I wondered if the effects for them differed from those I experienced. When I asked them their feelings about journaling Allie said, "It's a notebook where you write down your day and how it feels," and Sarah replied, "It's fun—I love to write, it makes me feel good." I asked the girls to do me a favor and combine two pen and paper techniques by writing an acrostic poem using the word "journal" (an acrostic poem is one in which each letter of a word represents the first letter in the line of the poem). As they showed me their poems, both apologized, saying they had filled in only some of the letters. I glanced down at the papers, and a speechless smile formed on my face. Their two partial poems slotted together perfectly—just as a key fits into a lock—making the complete poem.

J	just for you
O	one day at a time
U	undivided attention
R	remember
N	nightly ritual
A	amazing secrets written
L	life

The girls intuitively filled in the individual letters that meant something to each of them personally. An unspoken synergy had collectively created a balanced, genuine, and innocent reflection of journaling. For me, to write is to experience a release or outpouring of my inner self, freely expressed—a gift to me.

MANDALA: THE COLORING MEDITATION

What is a mandala? In Sanskrit, *mandala* means "sacred circle." Mandalas have been used for centuries as aids in healing, their circular form helping to organize perception, thought, and physical responses in positive ways.

Impermanence

Recently my family visited our local Museum of Natural History and Science, where there was an exhibit of a mandala. A group of Buddhist monks had created the mandala using colored sand. It was beautifully and intricately done with an amazing attention to detail, truly a work of art. We gasped in disbelief when we heard that it would be destroyed when the exhibit was finished. In this tradition mandalas are temporary structures built of impermanent materials. These mandalas are deliberately destroyed to represent life's impermanence. Typically their sand is swept up after completion and poured into a nearby stream or river. Just like me riding in the back seat, this is a wonderful reminder of letting go.

Putting it into practice

I use mandalas in my practice of working with mothers and children. It provides a great way for issues that may be imbedded within the child to have a way of coming out—creative self-expression at its best. Start by either drawing your own circle or use a black and white template of a patterned circle. Let your child color in the pattern or create one of his own. Provide primary colors and allow him to choose whichever colors he wants to fill in the patterns. The colored mandala can be a helpful tool in diagnosing the emotional well-being of a person. The power of this circle is to establish order and to creates patterns the mind can understand. Kids love it. I describe it to them as a coloring meditation. The only rule is that they have to focus on their coloring, remaining silent while working on their mandala.

> You will find, as you look back on your life, that the moments that stand out are the moments when you have done things for others. — **Henry Drummond**

Service to others

This last summer, it became obviously clear that doing something that initially appeared as a chore or a "have to" ended up paying back in an unforeseen richness of experience. Focusing on others and not yourself provides a heart-felt opportunity to connect with spirit, learn lessons of compassion and non-judgment, all the while innocently practicing the mantra—"in giving of yourself you are truly the receiver."

Allie and Sarah were involved with a halfway house service project, working with women just released from prison. Their first morning I went along with them to make sure they could find their way to a place a little out of our neighborhood. All of us were all a little nervous that first morning, as we were completely out of our "hood," both physically and emotionally. How could my sweet daughters share meals and conversation with women who literally may have spent their previous night in prison? As a mother, it was a challenge to walk back out of the center and say, "See you this afternoon."

A place to get back on their feet

The founder and hands-on director, an Irish ex-cop turned nun, Sister Maureen, runs the center like a well-oiled machine—it's obvious she doesn't mess around. The center is several houses linked to create a common area, garden, bedrooms, and communal kitchen. The women who get the opportunity to come here keep it maintained as part of their commitment to change. This haven provides a comforting and sparkling clean home (I think it may be cleaner than my house) for these women as they put their lives back together and re-enter society.

Every day the girls came home with new stories to tell—sometimes we laughed and sometimes

we cried. We talked a lot about how these women's life circumstances—physical, sexual and mental abuse, drugs, alcohol, poverty and crime—were part of each of their lives. It was easy to understand how the women at the center became part of the never-ending cycle that contributed to their stay in prison.

After only a few days I knew all was well, as the girls didn't complain about going each morning, setting off with smoothies in hand and smiles on their face. It was becoming obvious how closely and intently they observed and soaked in this new experience. It was challenging to be involved with women who had so many troubles and yet so liberating to think that these women were now in a place to help them break their life's cycle of crime and abuse. As difficult as it seemed, there was hope. The girls became so fond of the women, and the women grew affectionate toward the girls. Together, they were teaching each other lessons of hardship and hope.

Not compassion through pity

Their connection was through compassion. Not compassion through pity, but instead a compassionate tenderness to ways in which they were allowed to share each other's experiences. Somehow they all found common ground, chatting about the latest *People Magazine*, or complaining about the humidity. These simple connectors allowed them to realize that even though they felt so opposite, their lives foreign to the others, they were reminded that on some level we are all connected. The women watched the girls eat a healthy packed lunch, amazed the girls would willingly eat carrots and enjoy them, while the girls listened to misfortune and suffering, stories the girls would never have known, teaching them to be aware of danger and consequences. They watched and listened and learned from each other.

Who's helping whom?

The couple of months passed quickly, and the girls finished their service project. A week or so later lingering on after dinner, we were talking about the girls summer experience. As I listened and watched their animated expressions I couldn't help stop and wonder who was helping whom in this experience? It allowed me to stand firm in the truth, "In giving of ourselves, we truly receive."

IDEAS OF HOW TO GIVE BACK

- **In your own home.** Sometimes starting at home is the simple answer. Pay attention to the needs of those nearest to you. Think of how you can nurture them in a simple everyday way—amazing things can happen.

- **Choose wisely.** It's easy to get overwhelmed with volunteering. Prioritize. You and your family come first; then put your energy into a passion that also gives back. Maybe it's volunteering to go on a campout with the Boy Scouts, teaching your favorite hobby to children or the elderly, or signing up to help in a place that brings you peace, such as a church or museum. Whatever you choose, make sure you enjoy it; don't offer up service from a place of guilt.

- **Reflect on.** What service have you been a part of in the past? What worked and what didn't? Build on lessons learned.

- **Donate money or time.** What works for you? Imagine if everyone who was able donated .5 percent of their income to those in need. Wonderful things could happen.

LET YOUR LIGHT SHINE

Our deepest fear is not that we are inadequate, our deepest fear is that we are powerful beyond measure. It is our light, not our darkness that most frightens us.

We ask ourselves who am I to be brilliant, gorgeous, talented, fabulous? Actually, who are you not to be? You are a child of God. Your playing small does not serve the world. There is nothing enlightened about shrinking so that other people won't feel insecure around you. We were born to make manifest the glory of God that is within us. It is not just in some of us; it is in everyone. And as we let our own light shine, we unconsciously give other people permission to do the same. As we are liberated from our own fear, our presence automatically liberates others. —**Marianne Williamson**

CREATING A PEACEFUL HOME

A protected haven

There is a distinct comfort in arriving home to a house that is simply in order. Add in the aroma of cooking or the scent of flowers, and it truly soothes body and soul. The home is a sacred dwelling, a protected haven to relax and recharge in a barefoot comfort, free from the outside world's stimulation. Creating a peaceful home is doable. Begin one room or corner at a time, whether you live in a one-bedroom apartment or a five-bedroom house.

A gathering place

Think of the gathering place in your home. Is it the kitchen, family room, or an outdoor space? A gathering place exists in every home. Once you find it, put your energy into creating this one room or space into a peaceful, comfortable and welcoming space—visually and sensually. What are some ways you can make this space more inviting? According to Denise Linn, author of *Sacred Space* and *Space Clearing A-Z*, "Things occur around us that cause fear and stress, so it's essential to have a place where we can be to reflect and reconnect." Locate this in your home, build a natural nest, and you will soothe body and mind. Here are some ideas to get you started:

Essential oils

I use essential oils every day to create an atmosphere. With either a spray bottle or a tiny machine that diffuses the oil (mixed with water), I create whatever environment I need. As the oils are released into the air it not only smells fantastic but I absorb their balancing properties when I breathe. Purifying lemon grass, soothing lavender, and uplifting orange, is the reason I use all kinds of essential oils. The use of essential oils dates back to biblical times, their effectiveness stands the test of time. They are Mother Earth's natural goodness, the "high-grade" fuel of a plant. Scientifically, essential oils hold the molecular structure to bind with our cells—creating more than just good smelling positive effects.

Create a space for your family

Think about your present space. Where is your family's favorite place to "hang out?" Once you've got it in mind—take some time to think it through from a practical standpoint, does the furniture arrangement work? Can you de-clutter the space? Does it get natural light? Does it have a view? Look for what this space has to offer and then take action. Dedicate a morning or afternoon to "redo" your space. That doesn't mean you have to go out and buy new things—it means thinking about what you already have and how it works for you in the best way. Simple things, such as turning off the TV, clearing clutter, rearranging a little furniture, and buying or cutting some fresh flowers, can make a huge difference.

Create a favorite spot for YOU

After establishing the family's favorite space, choose another. But this time, produce a restorative refugee for you. Lead by example, and your children (if they haven't already) may follow suit and create their own, too. Is it sitting in a comfortable chair, lying in bed, soaking in the tub? Find a nurturing special place is a gift to yourself that's too good to be left undiscovered. Creating different areas for different times and moods comes with thought and intention. Once done, remain mindful to your ever-changing needs. Recognize when these needs change and recreate spaces to meet them.

> *Creating different areas for different times and moods comes with thought and intention.*

Safe and secure

Creating a home that is secure and soothing can be a much-needed remedy to de-stress, feel removed and safe from the stimulation of the outside world. Our homes give us a place to just "be." It is in this place of "being" that we become open to discover the sacred space within us.

FINDING A QUIET STILL SPACE

Building a peaceful home within

In building a peaceful home, we effortlessly pass on the benefits to our children. Kids are like sponges. They absorb so much of what is around them, they reflect and become what they see, feel, and hear. Whether it is the interior of my physical home or the inner intimacy of my heart, I expect my kids to be and act as I am. Creating a spiritual peaceful home inside and out for them guides them along their way to building one of their own.

Finding a quiet space

Finding a Quiet Space is not only the title of my guided audio relaxation, it is a much need remedy for our internal home—our heart and mind. Teaching our children about how to become quiet for a few minutes in the simple act of thought or prayer helps them find this place.

Teaching children about creating space for thanks and grace

Children are pure and innocent, free from the clutter of the world, and instinctive in their ability to offer up gratitude and thanks each day. Show them how to relax and become quiet and still; maybe it's just a deep breath in and out before focusing their attention. Follow with gentle and heartfelt words of thankfulness, love, grace, patience, and compassion. Dedicate time each day. For my family, meals, waking up, and bedtime became a natural time of the day. Be creative and discover what works for you—take inspiration from centuries ago or from spontaneous thoughts. What are you thankful for? Who loves you? Whom do you love? What feels like grace in your life? Are you patient with yourself and others? It doesn't take much to get them started, and they are off. These quiet times soon become effortless and soothing.

> **UNCOVER THE GODDESS WITHIN**
>
> Michelangelo's David is based on the artistic discipline of *"disegno."* The origin of the word *segno di dio* in noi means **"the sign of God in us,"** much like our human soul is found deep within our physical body. We just need to chip away at our very own Godly essence to uncover the hidden splendor, revealing God's work—resting and anchored in our inner true self.

Songs of truth

Ancient and sacred hymn collections form the text known as the Upanishads. These texts make up the basis of India's religious system. They are known as "songs of truth." One of the main themes from the Upanishads is more Zen than Hindu. Eknath Easwaran speaks of this in his book, *Original Goodness*: "What is the light of man? Reality exists in all things, and to discover this we need to 'peel back' into our self, like peeling the layers of an onion."

TAKE THE TEST

For the essential oil to be medicinal, it needs to be pure. These oils are the highest grade of "fuel" from the plant. This simple test will tell you if your essential oils are pure or if base oils were added. Here's how:

- **Place a drop** or two of essential oil on a tissue.
- **Place the tissue** in an open-air area.
- **Eventually the oil** should completely evaporate, leaving no oily residue.

LOVE HAS NO LIMITS

Love is our true essence. Love has no limitations of caste, religion, race, or nationality. We are all beads strung together on the same thread of love. To awaken this unity—and to spread to others the love that is our inherent nature—is the true goal of human life.

— **Ammachi, "the hugging saint"**

DEEP LOVE FOR ONE ANOTHER

Finally, having the tools to create balance in our lives doesn't mean that we aren't going to come up against challenges. It means we are coming from a place of capacity to meet the unexpected, creating those "shock absorbers" that mean you have the capacity to bring yourself to those around you willingly, and with generosity. Infusing principles of spirit strengthens us, feeding us into our way of being until it becomes a daily part of our lives.

Most important of all, continue to show

deep love for each other, for love for each

other makes up for many of your faults.

God has given each of you some

special abilities be sure to use

them to help each other.

— 1 PETER 4:8-10

Chapter 7: What Feeds Your Spirit?

Q: *Why do I want to "feed my spirit"?*

A: I feel spirit, as the light in my soul, a divine spark of inner peace and strength, enabling me to carry on through difficult times. As I reconnect with this flame deep inside me it warms through me from the inside with feelings of security, self-confidence, and steadfastness. I feel it is essential to tend to and nourish this connection in creating a healthy and joy-filled life.

Q: *How do I go about connecting to and nurturing that inner part of me? And, sharing these with my child?*

A: In this chapter I describe proven methods for connecting with your spirit—unlocking your creative soul, doing vision work, playing like a child, spending time on your own, and finding quiet space in your mind through meditation or prayer—all of these clear out "clutter" of day-to-day living. These things work for me and can work for you and your children, helping you find a place of greater clarity and peace. I encourage you to incorporate time in everyday to connect with spirit and by teaching your child to honor and respect this connection to spirit it gives them a rock to anchor upon.

Q: *I did some volunteer work in the past and remember feeling drained afterwards. Is that how I am supposed to feel? I thought I would feel good.*

A: My advice is to choose your volunteer projects wisely as it's easy to get overwhelmed with volunteering. Prioritize. You and your family come first; then put your energy into a passion that also gives back. Maybe it's volunteering to go on a campout with the Boy Scouts, teaching your favorite hobby to children or the elderly, or signing up to help in a place that brings you peace, such as a church or museum. Whatever you choose, make sure you enjoy it; don't offer up service from a place of guilt. Remember to reflect back. What service have you been a part of in the past? What worked and what didn't? Build on lessons learned. Another way to contribute to society is to donate money. What works for you? Imagine if everyone who was able to donated .5 percent of their income to those in need. Wonderful things could happen.

Q: *I understand the importance of creating sacred space in our home as a much needed remedy to de-stress and provide a protected haven. Give me one of your favorite tips to use in creating a peaceful home.*

A: I use essential oils every day to create my own atmosphere. With either a spray bottle or a tiny machine that diffuses the oil (mixed with water), I create whatever environment I need. As the oils are released into the air, it not only smells fantastic but I absorb their balancing properties when I breathe: Purifying lemon grass, soothing lavender, and uplifting orange. The use of essential oils dates back to biblical times, and their effectiveness stands the test of time. They are Mother Earth's natural goodness, the "high-grade" fuel of a plant. Scientifically, essential oils hold the molecular structure to bind with our cells—creating more than just good smelling positive effects.

8

Motherhood

The foundation of a healthy lifestyle begins step by step, brick by brick. Building your solid foundation with small, simple, everyday choices creates a framework to withstand the ebbs and flows of a demanding, fast-paced lifestyle. As mothers, if we dedicate our energy and set our intention to creating a healthy lifestyle, we effortlessly pass on the benefits to our children. Kids are like thirsty sponges: They absorb everything around them. Children reflect and become what they see, feel and hear; and our modeling a healthy lifestyle guides them along the way to building one of their own. Therefore, by changing our own habits, we lay the foundation for ourselves and our children in creating generations of healthy families.

Motherhood is the reason I have entered this place of health and happiness; motherhood is the reason I need balance and receive joy. And so, in the end here are my five best pieces of advice on being a mom. They are the bricks that built my solid foundation on which I have built my life with my family. I hope that they may lend some inspiration to yours.

Enjoy

Speaking from my nursing background, I can say the initial stages of motherhood are classically known as the "honeymoon" phase. And it's true; motherhood provides endless opportunities for joy and happiness. So go ahead, take enormous pleasure in the "miracle" of your child and your family. From my personal experience, I can say motherhood passes very quickly. With two girls now thinking of what lies beyond high school and a son taller than I am, I can still remember a time when Sam was a newborn and Sarah and Allie were toddlers. I also remember that it was as if this baby and twin Zen masters had descended into my life to teach me the gift of patience. My days were so physically exhausting—caring for three children under four years old while my husband worked long hours was hard work. Time passed by as a blur. In fact, I am pretty sure I lost most contact with the real world for stretches of weeks at a time! However, in the midst of that physical tiredness and mental amnesia there were many moments of pure bliss. I remember a simply beautiful day at the park, Sam and I snuggled on a bench watching the girls happily playing, thinking to myself this was probably one of the best moments in my life. I only wish now I had known to focus on these types of magical moments more, and that when things really fell apart to have giggled more as I did in the back seat of the car driving down the road with Sam and Sarah. So, even if you are feeling scared because you feel you don't know what you are doing, or exhausted from one more trip to the grocery store, or overwhelmed with the nerve-wracking chaos that day-to-day living can bring, know that in all of this ordinary activity lies pure joy that only motherhood can bring.

- **Enchantment.** I encourage you to revel in the magic of motherhood. From the moment my babies entered into this world, and now as I am preparing for them to fly the coop, I have tried to appreciate every moment I can, even while trying to cope with those more difficult ones. I remind myself of all the goodness in my day as a mother and that precious moments are always available for the taking, if I am willing to notice them. Finding one is like buried treasure—a gem that makes you feel so rich.

- **Live like you are on vacation.** Think back to one of your best vacations. Recall how good it felt to be stress-free and smiling, enjoying yourself and watching your kids move through their days with abandon. Stop "fighting through" a long day and start enjoying the precious moments. And, just as you take care of you on vacation, do this more often—live in vacation mode more often.

- **Put down the list.** Remember life as a mother isn't just about a to-do list; sometimes it's about putting the list down.

- **Practice present moment.** The practice of being mindful of the moment you are experiencing right now. Focus your thoughts and/or actions on ONE thing at a time. Start small, gradually allowing this simple but effective Zen practice to become a welcome habit in your every day. Whether I am folding the laundry, washing a dish, or leading a meeting—if I focus my attention on the task at hand, I am meditating.

- **Lighten up.** When I look back at my life as a mother, if I look through a lens of compassion and understanding, and humor, every action or thought turns into a potential way into loving kindness. Your reactions are your choice—you can get upset, or you can laugh. Which one will bring more joy?

CALM IN CHAOS

Motherhood can sometimes feel like a continual series of interruptions. As a mother, your thoughts, tasks, almost everything and anything you do can feel fragmented. It can seem like everyone wants your attention at once: the ringing cell, the tug on your sleeve, the yell from upstairs, "Mom, where's my . . . "

Calm in the chaos

Last autumn driving through the rolling flint hills of eastern Kansas for Thanksgiving, we crossed over the bridge leading to my small hometown where the banks of the Kansas River seemed wider than they did when I was a child. As I walked through my front door, I was met with the scent of delicious cooking and the warmth in my parents' faces, combined with their loving hugs instantly transported me back to the time of my youth. Even though I am a grown woman with a family of my own, I was amazed at how quickly I felt twelve years old again.

Your reactions are your choice—you can get upset, or you can laugh. Which one will bring more joy?

As the day progressed, my entire extended family arrived in stages, our numbers adding up to about thirty people and five dogs. My mother, who is the definition of grounded and calm, has always had a way of being a natural reflection of what it is to be centered and at peace. I don't think she particularly knows about the concept of present moment, or mindfulness. But, her way of being is truly an innate skill, which she calls upon every day, honed from fifty years of experience in raising nine children. A buzz of chatting, laughing, children running, dogs barking, and all sorts of chaos brought back the memory of life in a big family, with my mom standing in the center of it all—as a centripetal force, present, in the moment. How to bring more calm into every day:

· **Self-care.** Carve out time everyday for self-care using tools of yoga, breathing, and relaxation. Maybe it's a healing hobby that allows you to lose track of time on the clock, or it's time spent in a stress-free space. Whatever you choose—make it a priority, everyday.

· **Alternative therapies.** Get that "ooh-la-la" feeling with a body massage, and everyone feels the repercussions of your time spent nurturing you. Why not try a new therapy? Sometimes it feels easier to stay with what you know, but there are so many wonderful practices to discover. Who knows? Your new favorite alternative practitioner may be just around the corner.

· **Quiet space every day.** Replenish your reservoir by spending time alone each day. Spend time in the restorative refuge dedicated for you. What sounds like you—soaking in the tub, a chair in the garden, or a favorite perch with a view?

Ritual

Everyday routine—babies and children need it, and so do you. This doesn't mean maintaining a drill sergeant's schedule; it means having a general framework for the day. Establish consistency. Create routines around things such as meal times and bedtimes. In doing this, you create predictable security. These rituals go on to build foundations of security and trust that last a lifetime.

I asked my mom about her secrets in raising nine children, and she said, "Three things really: Love, routine/ritual, and discipline are the basic principles your father and I used in raising all of you." Try out some of these ideas to either re-establish routines already in place or use as inspiration to create some new rituals and lay the groundwork for your family:

- **A safe vessel.** Kids need to talk. They need to feel safe and worthy in the knowledge that what they will say is important to hear. They need to be given the opportunity to speak freely, clear the day, and share their news. I always capitalize on my time in the car—and it has become a welcomed habit. When I open the car door, instantaneously the mood is available—it's a capsule in time. There are no distractions. I turn off my radio and phone, and with a few deep breaths, make a place for the peaceful silence that a few deep breaths can bring. Whether I am alone or have my children in the car—it becomes a quiet and uninterrupted space for them to talk and me to listen.

- **Bedtime ritual.** When our kids were young we always had a bedtime ritual. Bath and pajamas, snack, then upstairs into bed for a story, snuggle, and a goodnight prayer. This was my children's nightly routine and similar to the ritual from my own childhood. My teenagers have now established their own evening routine which keeps them in sync with their life of studying, activities and socializing. I feel that childhood routine, gave my kids guidelines and structure that laid the foundation for them to now create their own habits. Bedtime routines have survived the test of time, giving kids a real sense of what to expect and what's expected of them. For us it works like a dream.

- **Family vacation.** On a recent family trip to Central America, we explored new territory on a hike in the mountains. Sam led us (and I brought up the rear) on a several hour trek, up and down inclines through dense jungle. Arriving at our destination we found a magical scene—a waterfall with its own lagoon. Exhausted from the hours on the trail, it felt as if I had stepped into a Shangri-la. We spent the afternoon swimming and relaxing with our picnic lunch, soaking in the magic. I felt enormous gratitude to spend time and be re-acquainted with my closest comrades, my family. And, it provided a much needed rekindling of our energy, and time to reconnect to last us long enough until the next vacation.

Lessons learned

The roles and responsibilities under the job title of "mother" are so vast, such an endless list; it is unlikely anyone would ever knowingly sign up for the job. However, this great effort can reward us with the most fulfilling moments of our lives. I feel our children bring lessons. I was given the gift of twin daughters and a son. Each of them is unique—and as they grow, I grow, too, in understanding their strengths and weaknesses, learning to respect each of them as individuals, for their own divine essence and special gifts. How do I learn from my children?

- **Uncover their gifts.** Whether it's creating a vision board with your child, caring for the environment together or sharing a bedtime visualization—help your child uncover his unique gifts. In offering up any idea, allow him to choose what works for him.

- **Let them fail.** It can be a challenge to let your child find his own way, but when I can step back and allow my kids to make their own choices—which succeed or fail—and learn to understand what their gifts are, compassion and understanding flow in. My kids have learned some of their most powerful lessons through failure.

- **Honor your child.** Honor your children. I respect the diversity between each of my children and I love to bring attention to their unique gifts. Give them permission to allow their gifts to shine through, be grateful for their abilities and teach them not to compare themselves against others. As Mother Theresa stated so beautifully, "You can do what I can't do. I can do what you can't do. Together we can do something beautiful for God."

- **Watch and learn.** I describe all three of my children as "being comfortable in their own skin." For me this describes the essence in living a balanced life. Whether that means they are confident in themselves within the influence of friends, awareness of what they ate and how it made them feel, or knowing how to juggle the demands of school, activities, and socializing. Each of them is comfortable spending time alone, and all three crave their quiet "me time," often explaining to friends they need some time on their own to relax and recharge.

Love

Mother and child have a bond that is natural and deeply rooted. It is an intuitive connection to care for a child who came into this world without any instructions. As natural as motherhood can be—it will challenge you to stretch outside of any boundary you thought humanly possible; stressed-out, frustrated and overwhelmed.

If you look in the yogic texts, they say that two of the highest forms of yoga are being in a marriage and having children: It's the ultimate mirror you hold up. Being a mother gives us the opportunity in every moment of our day to look with softened eyes and heart to be the expression of our best self. How do I love my child even more?

- **Love what you do.** Whether that means driving my child to a baseball practice, teaching my child how to read a food label and eat more foods without a label, listening with eyes and ears and heart to a story that needs to be told, or loving my husband, I love what I do.

- **Be kind.** Speaking kind and honest words begins within our own family. Kids are like sponges. They absorb so much of what is around them, they reflect and become what they see, feel, and hear and I expect my kids to be and act as I am.

- **Feel good from the inside out.** When our families feel good on the inside, we mothers feel the love, too. I have a great friend who always says, as a mom you are only as happy as your unhappiest child. Think about how good you feel when your kids, your whole family are happy and healthy. Be the creator of a healthy and happy ebb and flow for your family—you are the moon driving the tide.

Come back to the essence

As a mother, I rely on my intuitive feeling, my knowingness of unconditional love and respect, resting confident in nurturing my children in a healthy and happy lifestyle brings home the instinctual calling of how to care for a child who came into this world without any instructions. Actually, my role as a mother has allowed me to open up and caused the formation of a person I didn't know existed. It has dug down into the depths of me and extracted a deeper love, given me more compassion and a higher purpose in nurturing a child. This unfolding has made me more beautiful and more vulnerable than ever before.

Where do you place value?

The world defines success as reflected in money, prestige, or academia. But a well-centered child who grows into a contributing adult, who creates a better world?—priceless. Society gives recognition or applause for a well-designed skyscraper or a beautiful movie star but gives little notice to parents for their work in guiding and nurturing a child's soul. Recognize the scope of motherhood with all of its responsibility and deep rewards. I am not saying mothers are responsible for raising perfect children—but kids who know the difference between right and wrong, children with values of compassion, honesty, and integrity. Not for one minute is this satisfying role a waste of my time or gifts. It is right at the heart of the most prestigious and challenging jobs I can undertake.

Touchstones for a healthy self and a healthy child

Through the touchstones of caring for my body, mind and soul—whether it's my ritual of self-care through yoga and meditation, using an everyday task, such as cooking, as a mindful meditation, buying organic milk and meat, tapping into creative self-expression through music, or encouraging my kids to tap into their talents—these avenues become my guide posts, my touchstones empowering me, and hopefully empowering you on our journey through motherhood.

As the endless and often thankless job of being a mother can at times feel next to impossible, my hope is that the stories, ideas and suggestions through out this book reach out as a helping hand, a book you can dip into when ever you need a fresh idea or boost of encouragement.

My pearls

For me, a pearl holds feminine, luminous magic. This original tiny grain of sand is pure, sacred, and innocent, securely protected from harm's way while allowed to grow in the image of its mother's shining interior. I hold this as an image of my precious children and the sacredness of my own well-being.

This life of true wellbeing begins from that inner place, living from the inside out. As I embrace this way of life it nurtures the precious jewel of my own wellbeing and those pearls that are my children. My healthy actions speak louder than any words—health and happiness spontaneously radiate out to my children effortlessly nurturing them in a healthy lifestyle.

I hope you know that the "gems" I have offered you in this book have been polished from decades of knowledge and experience, encased in years of personal and professional dedication, and layered with unconditional love. In staying true to living a healthy, happy, and joyful life, a continual work-in-progress exists. A removal of ordinary, everyday frustrations; irritations and disappointments are replaced with a deep self-confidence, trust, and faith in this way of living for myself and my children. I remain hopeful that my message, this way of healthy living, will lead us all into a newly alive, ever-evolving, happier and brighter future for generations to come.

Your children are not your children. They are the sons and daughters of Life's longing for itself. They come through you but not from you, and though they are with you yet they belong not to you.

You may give them your love but not your thoughts, for they have their own thoughts. You may house their bodies but not their souls, for their souls dwell in the house of tomorrow, which you cannot visit, not even in your dreams. You may strive to be like them, but seek not to make them like you. For life goes not backward nor tarries with yesterday. You are the bows from which your children as living arrows are sent forth.

The archer sees the mark upon the path of the infinite, and He bends you with His might that His arrows may go swift and far. Let your bending in the Archer's hand be for gladness; For even as He loves the arrow that flies, so He loves also the bow that is stable.

— Kahlil Gibran, *The Prophet*

In staying true to living a healthy, happy, and

joyful life, a continual work-in-progress exists.

A removal of ordinary, everyday frustrations;

irritations and disappointments are replaced

with a deep self-confidence, trust, and faith in

this way of living for myself and my children.

I remain hopeful that my message, this way of

healthy living, will lead us all into a newly alive,

ever-evolving, happier and brighter future

for generations to come.

Chapter 8: Motherhood

Q: *I agree that motherhood can feel like a continual series of interruptions. My life feels fragmented with everyone vying for my attention. What can I do to stay calm?*

A: Your reactions are your choice. You can get upset, or you can laugh. Which one will bring you more joy? I also practice being in the present moment. The practice of being mindful of the moment you are experiencing right now. Focus your thoughts and/or actions on ONE thing at a time. Whether I am folding the laundry, washing a dish, or leading a meeting—if I focus my attention on the task at hand—I am staying calm and in the moment.

Q: *Everyone says a ritual is so important for children. Can you tell me why?*

A: I feel an everyday routine is something babies and children need, and so do you. This doesn't mean maintaining a drill sergeant's schedule; it means having a general framework for the day. Establish consistency. Create routines around things such as meal times and bedtimes. In doing this, you create predictable security. These rituals go on to build foundations of security and trust that last a lifetime.

Q: *If you had to pass down one lesson that you have learned through your role as a mother, what would that be?*

A: Many lessons are continually being learned for me, but if I were to choose one, I would say—watch and learn. I describe all three of my children as "being comfortable in their own skin." For me, this describes the essence in living a balanced life. Whether that means they are confident in themselves within the influence of friends, awareness of what they ate and how it made them feel, or knowing how to juggle the demands of school, activities, and socializing. Each of them is comfortable spending time alone, and all three crave their quiet "me time," often explaining to friends they need some time on their own to relax and recharge. Watching them grow and learn is a beautiful experience.

Q: *Can you give me one final tip about being a mom?*

A: As a mother, I rely on my intuition and unconditional love and respect to confidently nurture my children in a healthy and happy lifestyle. For me, my role as a mother has allowed me to open up and caused the formation of a person I didn't know existed. It has dug down into the depths of me and extracted a deeper love, given me more compassion and a higher purpose in nurturing a child. This unfolding has made me more beautiful and more vulnerable than ever before.

Resources

Acupuncture

American Academy of Medical Acupuncture. This is a physician organization promoting the use of acupuncture with western medical training. **medicalacupuncture.org**

Ayurveda

The Ayurvedic Institute, in the foothills of northeast Albuquerque, is recognized as a leading Ayurvedic school and Ayurveda health spa outside of India. It was established in 1984 to teach the traditional Ayurvedic medicine of India and to provide these ancient therapies. **ayurveda.com**

Andrew Weil, M.D.

This man has been an inspiration to my work for two decades. He offers endless information for healthy living based on the philosophy of integrative medicine through his numerous books, online resources, and newsletters. Dr. Weil is an internationally recognized expert for his views on leading a healthy lifestyle, his philosophy of healthy aging, and the future of medicine and health care. His site is a resource for education, information, products, services and philanthropic contributions based on the principles of integrative medicine. **drweil.com**

Deepak Chopra, M.D.

Deepak Chopra continues to transform our understanding of the meaning of health. *Time* magazine calls him "the poet-prophet of alternative medicine." His site has Q & A dialogue, as well as numerous educational seminars, products, services and books on Ayurveda. **chopra.com**

CranioSacral Therapy

The Upledger Institute is a health resource center located in Palm Beach Gardens, Florida. **upledger.com**

Homeopathic Educational Services

Homeopathic Educational Services is a great source for homeopathy. It has books, tapes research, medicines, and software. **homeopathic.com**

Flower Essences

Flower essences in a bottle, tagged as yoga in a bottle. "Rescue Remedy has become every woman's emotional ally for its calming and centering energy providing unconditional support during demanding times." Personally, I have been using Rescue Remedy for the past twenty years for my family and myself. **rescueremedy.com**

ALLERGIES

American Academy of Allergy Asthma and Immunology.

Sign up to receive a free, weekly "Allergy Gram" via e-mail, which shows the latest pollen counts in their areas and explains the meaning of the pollen count. **allergy-info.com**

The Center for Disease Control and Prevention

The Center for Disease Control and Prevention has a great deal of info on allergy basics, common triggers, and info for specific groups. **cdc.gov/asthma**

Allergy Management

This website, through the CDC, is info for children at different age groups, teaching them how to manage their allergy symptoms and the main page has allergy info for the day, air quality conditions and the like. **airnow.gov**

Allergy Capitals

This is a website that gives the "Allergy Capitals" of the U.S., at the Allergy and Asthma Foundation of America. **aafa.org**

BODY PRODUCTS

Trillium Organics

These organic products are the best I have found. The body oil, soap, and scrub are infused with specific essential oils to create whatever mood is needed to keep your body in balance. **trilliumorganics.com**

GOING GREEN

Local Harvest

This website allows you to zoom in on your hometown and find local farmers' markets, grocers that sell locally grown goods, and restaurant that serve locally grown foods. **localharvest.org**

Wisconsin Department of Natural Resources

This is the website for the Wisconsin Department of Natural Resources—check out their Environmental Education for Kids section. It's very informative. It teaches kids about endangered species, recycling, and global warming, among many other things. **dnr.state.wi.us**

Earth 911

This site explains where, how, and why to recycle in great detail, a one-stop shop for recycling info. Just type in your zip code, and it tells you where to recycle. **earth911.com**

Computer Recycling Center

This non-profit site, Computer Recycling Center and Computers for Education, takes all computers, technology, network, telephone, test equipment, and cell phones. **crc.org**

Junk Mail Elimination

Eliminate junk mail and "reclaim your mailbox." The average adult receives 41 pounds of junk mail each year. This organization stops 80 to 95 percent of unwanted catalogues and junk mail for you. They also donate a third of the $41 fee to a charity of your choice. **41Pounds.org**

Healthy Child Healthy World

Non-profit organization. The products this company uses every day impact the world we live in. Learn how to create a safer environment for your child. **healthychild.org**

Green Dimes

For $20, this group will keep your name off mailing lists for at least five years. Plus, GreenDimes will plant up to ten trees on your behalf. **greendimes.com**

Direct Marking Association

You remove your name from many mailing lists for free.

Catalog Choice

Sign yourself up for free and get off catalog mailing lists. **catalogchoice.org**

NCCAM

The National Center for Complementary and Alternative Medicine. A good site for all kinds of information regarding alternative medicine. **nccam.nih.gov**

Dr. Alan Greene, M.D.

Dr. Alan Greene, "America's favorite pediatrician," provides a stellar website with thousands of articles, videos, and illustrations for parents. **drgreene.com**

Mayo Clinic

The thing about the Mayo Clinic site is it allows you to input your interest and then receive email updates on those topics. **mayoclinic.com**

Medline Plus

This site has comprehensive data on any health condition. It is operated by the U.S. National Library and offers encyclopedic background on all diseases, definitions of medical terms and referrals to organizations that deal with specific illnesses. **medlineplus.gov**

Kids Health

This site provides three levels of advice for parents, children, and teenagers, and it's easy to read. **kidshealth.org**

About The Author

This book is the result of a talented team. Let me say thank you with deepest gratitude:

To Lam, my friend and surgeon and fabulous editor—it's been such good fun.

To the team at Bright Sky Press—Lucy, Ellen, and Rue, thank you for believing in me.

To Karen Walrond, for the beautiful images for this book, your natural talent is such a gift.
Photos appearing on pages 10, 20, 80, 82, 98, 114, 121, 128, 134, 136, 144

To Karen Sachar, you and your photographs are equally treasured.
Photos appearing on pages 24, 36, 63, 84, 154, 158, 163

To Mike, a true artist can listen and interpret. Your drawings bring life to my understanding of how yoga should feel. I am in gratitude of your ability.

To Wyn, your talent is a reflection of the beautiful design of this book, and I am grateful.

To Michelle, Laurie, Susan, and Monica your diligence and commitment have surrounded me with support, kindling this dream into reality.

To mom and dad, thanks for being such great parents.

To Allie, Sarah, and Sam,
Thanks for all of the great material. I love each of you more everyday.

To my husband Ron, your unconditional love and support allow me to be my best.

About The Author

Through her various roles as an ICU nurse, mother of three, yoga instructor, and author, Elizabeth believes we can create a healthier, happier way of being from the inside out and raise families who care—about themselves, about each other, and about the world around them. As spokesperson for healthy living, an educational partner for Andrew Weil's *weilbaby.com*, and through *elizabethirvine.com*, she reaches out to millions of readers. The author of *A Moment's Peace: Creating Calm Amidst Chaos*, she lives with her family in Houston, Texas.

To follow her blog, access free guided relaxation podcasts, and more: **elizabethirvine.com.** A percentage of proceeds from the sale of this book supports charities for women and children.